WHAT'S YOUR DOSHA, BABY?

LISA MARIE COFFEY is a lifestyle and relationship expert who appears frequently on television and radio talk shows and contributes to various publications with her unique and timely approach to family, relationships, and spiritual issues. She is the author of *Getting There with Grace: Simple Exercises for Experiencing Joy, Getting There!: 9 Ways to Help Your Kids Learn What Matters Most in Life,* and the coauthor of *The Healthy Family Handbook.* Coffey lives in the Los Angeles area with her husband and her two sons. Her Web address is www.coffeytalk.com.

Learn more about Ayurveda and join our online community by visiting www.whatsyourdosha.com. There you will find all the latest resource and contact information for Ayurvedic organizations so that you may further your study.

Lisa Marie Coffey can be reached via e-mail at DoshaDiva@aol.com.

Lisa Marie Coffey

Foreword by Dr. Vasant Lad

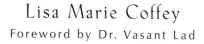

WHAT'S YOUR DOSHA, BABY?

Discover the Vedic Way

for Compatibility

in Life and Love

MARLOWE & COMPANY
NEW YORK

To Greg
Whose Pitta warms my Vata
And whose love warms my heart

.

CONTENTS

Foreword

AYURVEDA TEACHES THAT human life consists of relationships. Whether it is the relationship between an individual and the environment, between a man and a woman, between two friends, or between body, mind, and consciousness, the ancient wisdom of Ayurveda shows us how to live life in harmony.

In order to have healthy relationships, we must first understand ourselves and how we work. We can get a great deal of insight by looking at the balance of our *doshas* (*Vata*, *Pitta*, and *Kapha*), also called our *prakruti*, which is like a fingerprint because it's unique to each one of us. The ways in which *Vata*, *Pitta*, and *Kapha* express themselves in our bodies and minds defines our individuality—our specific sensitivities, likes and dislikes, and temperaments. We can use our *doshas* as a mirror to help us look at ourselves and see "what is," or what we actually are: living, dynamic beings subject to change. That is reality. Many of us spend our time looking at what "should be" or "would be" or "could be," which is all an illusion. Reality demands awareness, and in that awareness you will find compassion, love, and freedom. Awareness allows you to experience who you really are and to blossom.

Before you jump into the river of relationships, you must be absolutely clear about your mental status. You must ask yourself whether it is loneliness, fear, or anxiety that is making you fall into a particular relationship or clarity, compassion, and love. It is absolutely true that like attracts like. When two lonely individuals are attracted to each other, they fall into a relationship and mechanically repeat,

"I love you, I love you." But when their loneliness disappears, the relationship falls apart. So you need to be very aware of how you feel before entering into a relationship. A healthy relationship consists of clarity, compassion, understanding, and love for one another. A relationship like this is valuable and healing for both partners. It allows us to experience intimacy and unity because it is free from fear.

In April 2003 the Ayurvedic Institute was offering a wonderful seminar on relationships and it was there that I met Lisa Marie Coffey. She personally handed me the manuscript of her book *What's Your Dosha, Baby?* I read it and it deeply touched my heart. In this charming, loving book, Lisa brings Ayurvedic principles to a practical level in our lives. She shows how we can use our relationships as a mirror to watch ourselves and learn about ourselves. Relationships are the school of our daily lives, where we learn a great deal about our natures. This book will go a long way toward helping you better understand yourself in your daily relationships and will definitely inspire happiness and healing in our togetherness.

Love and light,

Vasant Lad, MASc
The Ayurvedic Institute
Albuquerque, NM

INTRODUCTION

Ask anyone and you'll get the same answer: What's the most important thing in life? Love! We want to be in love, and we want that love to last. So how do we go about finding that one person to share our lives with? And how do we live happily ever after with that person, once we find him or her?

There are many ways of looking at our compatibility with other people—such as the Mars/Venus theories and the Love Signs system based on astrology, among others. But long before any of these formulas were even a twinkle in the cosmos, philosophers and scientists in ancient India devised a system of health care called Ayurveda, or "the science of life." Within this holistic system lies everything we need to know about love.

Ayurveda explains the nature of everything in the universe. It is a compelling way of looking at all of life: its physical, emotional, mental, and spiritual aspects. Ayurveda "types" people according to their physical features and personality traits. Ayurveda tells us how we "tick," and how we relate to the rest of the world, including the other people in it!

Once we understand the basics of Ayurveda, we see that we can get along with anyone. There are no "bad" matches! So, whether you want to end the squabbling with your mate, you're having a hard time with your boss, or your boyfriend just won't commit, with this system of ancient Indian love matches, you'll find ways to make the relationship work.

It is impossible to go through this life alone. We all have relationships, people in our lives we interact with. The purpose of those relationships is to help us learn and grow. And more than that, the purpose of any relationship is to help us learn more about ourselves and who we really are.

When we understand who we are, and why we are here, everything seems to fall into place. We're happier and more content, and we feel our connection to the universe. We attract like-minded people into our lives and our relationships become stronger.

According to Ayurvedic wisdom, there are four basic principles of life; these are discussed in the Upanishads, the sacred texts upon which Hinduism is built. These principles form the foundation of Ayurveda and can be used to help us understand the role our relationships play in our lives.

There is an organizing power in the universe. The universe is intelligent and creates harmony. There are no accidents or coincidences. Nothing is random. Everything happens for a reason.

What does this mean for us? The people who are in our lives are there on purpose. What can we learn from them? How can we help them?

Everything that exists is living. Everything and everyone is made up of *prakriti* (material) and *purusha* (spirit). We vibrate with the life force inside us and all around us.

What does this mean for us? A relationship has a life of its own. How does a particular relationship serve us? How can it serve the world? How long is it meant to last?

All existence is interconnected. Everything in the universe, every pebble, bird, person, rainbow, is connected to every other thing in the universe. There is no separation between us.

What does this mean for us? We are all connected in some way, shape, or form. So, anything we do to another person, we do to ourselves. We need to be aware of feelings and emotions in a relationship and not cause any harm to each other.

The essence of everything is part of That—the Divine Creative Force. We are connected to each other and connected to the Whole, All That There Is, at the same time.

What does this mean for us? Our actions have repercussions that resonate in the universe. When we're happy and in love, that love increases the energy around us. It's contagious! Healthy relationships are essential to the health of the whole planet.

As important as our relationships are to us, how much time and effort do we really put into them? So often we go about living our lives and expect that another person either fits into that picture or doesn't. But we each have needs, temperaments, and ideas about how we like things to be. When we better understand ourselves and each other, we can focus on what is important and what makes a relationship work.

When I first learned about Ayurveda, I was impressed with how simple and clear it made everything to me. The whole system just makes sense, and you can apply it to anything in your life! I've read lots of books about Ayurveda and even more books on relationships, but I've never come across one book that applied this age-old system to our very modern-day relationships. So I decided to work it out myself, and that is how this book came to be.

Because Ayurveda sees people as three different mind-body types, or *doshas,* there are basically nine different "Love Matches." Of course, in reality, there is an infinite number of combinations, because no two people are exactly alike, but we've got to keep the numbers manageable here! Once you find out your particular dosha (see Chapter 1), and the dosha of the person with whom you are in relationship, you can look up the chapter that corresponds to the two of you. There you'll find clues to how you interact with each other, your communication styles (both physical and emotional), and instinctual preferences regarding food, travel, lifestyle, and work, among other areas. This system shows us how we can please each other and ourselves at the same time. It shows us how we can live in harmony with those around us by recognizing a person's natural qualities and bringing more love into the world.

If you are looking to understand or strengthen a relationship with someone other than your mate—say, a colleague, friend, or child—subsequent chapters will help you with that, too. And because we all have a unique relationship with our environment, I have included a chapter on that, as well. Through your use of space and color, you can create an environment where you feel inspired and blissful.

In addition to Ayurveda, the Vedic texts are filled with wisdom that we can use in all aspects of our relationships. There are ways that we can flow with universal energy to live healthier and happier lives. In this book we will explore the fundamentals of the ancient arts of mantra, tantra, yoga, and Jyotish, and you will learn how they can all teach you more about yourself. Growth is one of the fundamental laws of nature. When we learn and grow, we are not only helping ourselves, we are helping the whole world.

Love is an amazing phenomenon—it's the reason that all of us are here. It's worth our study, our attention. Why are we attracted to the people we are attracted to? Why is it that we feel as if we "can't help" who we fall in love with? What is the chemistry that draws us to certain people?

We may never figure ourselves out. Or maybe we already have. Maybe the ancient texts are right and all the answers we will ever need are available to us now . . . we just need to keep learning and growing until we finally "get it."

One thing's for sure. Finding love and connection is one of the most important—and pleasurable—things we do in our lives. My hope is that this book, with its ancient Indian secrets for keeping love burning bright, will not only help you in your process of self-discovery, but enable you to find and nourish the love matches of your dreams. I also hope that this book will help you better understand and accept people for who they are, which will not only bring you closer to your friends and family, but will also encourage productive and creative ventures with your associates and coworkers. We're all in this together, and we each have something wonderful to contribute.

WHAT'S YOUR
DOSHA, BABY?

MIND & BODY:
WHAT'S YOUR DOSHA, BABY?

Love is the one constant in the universe.
Love is from the infinite and
will be until eternity.
—RUMI

AYURVEDA EXPLAINS THAT human beings, like the universe, are made up of each of the five elements (air, space, fire, water, and earth) and the soul. Therefore, our bodies are microcosms of the universe within itself.

How are these elements expressed in our bodies? Air is inhaled when we breathe, and it pumps the blood through our systems to keep us alive. Space is in the hollow cavities of our bodies, and we require space to move around. Fire is the part of our digestive systems that helps to break down the food we eat and burn calories to give us energy. Water composes about two-thirds of our bodies, and we need water to survive. Earth is in our bones and our vital minerals that keep us healthy.

These elements, in their biological form, are known as doshas: Vata, Pitta, and Kapha. Vata is made up of a combination of air and space. Pitta is a combination of fire and water. Kapha is made up of earth and water.

Every activity and function of our minds and bodies is dependent upon the balanced or unbalanced state of our doshas.

Because we all have all of the elements in our bodies, we all have each of the doshas, as well. But every one of us is born with a unique, individual balance of these doshas. So, no two of us are alike! The idea is to find what your own special combination of doshas is and to work to keep them in balance so that you stay in radiant health, mentally, emotionally, and physically. Once you have figured out your own dominant dosha—and your mate's, or potential mate's—you can read up on how to make the most of your particular love match. If you don't already have a partner, the information in this book can help you decide which dosha might make the best love match for you. Just remember: There's no such thing as a bad match!

Just about everything can be classified by its dominant dosha. Here are a few examples of the ways Vata, Pitta, and Kapha are expressed in the world around us. See if you can begin to guess which dosha you are.

VATA	PITTA	KAPHA
gazelle	tiger	elephant
hummingbird	eagle	swan
stars	sun	moon
bamboo	pine	oak
violin	cello	bass
sand	clay	mud
orchid	rose	chrysanthemum
emu	kangaroo	koala
hurricane	volcano	avalanche

Even film and literary characters can be described by their dominant doshas. Here are a few to get you thinking!

VATA	PITTA	KAPHA
Scarlett O'Hara	Rhett Butler	Melanie Hamilton
Peter Pan	Captain Hook	Wendy
Olive Oyl	Popeye	Bluto
Tigger	Rabbit	Winnie-the-Pooh
Ace Ventura	Erin Brockovich	The Godfather
Snoopy	Lucy	Charlie Brown

By now you may have guessed what your own dominant dosha is, but I've devised a little quiz to help you be sure. There are two sections: one for the body and one for the mind. This will help you better define your dosha when you finish. Read the statements and circle the ones that are true for you (or seem to best describe you). None of the statements are *too* personal, so you should be able to answer for someone you know fairly well, too. Obviously, there are many more attributes to each dosha (and you will read about some in the course of this book), but the traits on this list are a good representation. When you have finished, add up your scores for each dosha category. Keep in mind that although all three doshas express themselves in some way in everyone, for most people, one or two are dominant.

WHAT'S MY DOSHA?
QUIZ

CIRCLE A, B, OR C to answer the following questions; choose whichever you think best describes you and your personality.

BODY

1. My least favorite kind of weather is
   a. cold weather
   b. hot weather
   c. damp weather

2.
   a. My hands and feet tend to be cold
   b. My hands are usually warm
   c. My hands are usually cool

3.
   a. My weight is below average for my build
   b. My weight is average for my build
   c. My weight is above average for my build

4.
   a. I tend to lose weight easily
   b. I maintain my weight easily
   c. I gain weight easily

5.
   a. My skin tends to be dry and rough, especially in winter
   b. My skin is soft and ruddy
   c. My skin is oily and moist

6. The most prominent feature about my hair is that
    a. it tends to be dry
    b. it's fine, thin, reddish, or prematurely gray
    c. it's thick and wavy

7.
    a. I walk quickly, more quickly than others
    b. I have a determined walk, just to get where I'm going
    c. My walk is slow and steady, a more leisurely pace

8.
    a. I like to be active, "on the go"; it's sometimes hard to sit still
    b. I enjoy physical activities with a purpose, especially competitive ones
    c. I like leisurely activities best

9. On a daily basis
    a. my appetite varies
    b. I am uncomfortable skipping meals
    c. I like to eat but can skip meals easily

10.
    a. I tend to eat quickly; I have a delicate digestion
    b. I have a strong digestion; I can eat almost anything
    c. I eat and digest slowly

11.
    a. I get worn out easily
    b. I am fairly strong and can handle various physical activities
    c. I have good stamina and a steady energy level

12.
- **a.** I am fairly flexible
- **b.** I am fairly muscular
- **c.** I am fairly solid and big-boned

MIND

13. When conflicts arise,
- **a.** I can be anxious and restless
- **b.** I can become intense and irritable
- **c.** I can get lazy or depressed

14.
- **a.** My moods change quickly
- **b.** My moods change slowly
- **c.** My moods are mostly steady

15.
- **a.** Under stress, I am easily excited
- **b.** Under stress, I can be angry or critical
- **c.** I'm pretty easygoing; it takes a lot to stress me out

16. The most prominent feature of my personality is that
- **a.** I am creative, imaginative
- **b.** I am intelligent, efficient, a perfectionist
- **c.** I am caring, calm, patient

17.
- **a.** I have lots of ideas and change my mind about things easily
- **b.** I gather lots of facts before forming an opinion
- **c.** I am stubborn; I make up my mind quickly and don't change my mind often

18.
- **a.** I have a short attention span
- **b.** I am detail-oriented and can focus for long periods of time
- **c.** I am a "big-picture" person and can focus for long periods of time

19.
- **a.** I learn quickly and forget quickly
- **b.** I have a good general memory
- **c.** I learn slowly and have a good long-term memory

20.
- **a.** I am good at getting things started but not necessarily at finishing them
- **b.** I am very organized and will see a project through from start to finish
- **c.** I may need help getting things started, but I am good at getting things accomplished

21.
- **a.** I tend to make and change friends often
- **b.** Most of my friends are work-related and change when I change jobs
- **c.** My friendships are long-lasting and sincere

22.
- **a.** I like to shop and often spend too much money
- **b.** I don't like to spend money, except on special items
- **c.** I prefer not to spend at all; I'm good at saving money

23.

    a. I have difficulty falling or staying asleep

    b. I sleep well, for an average length of time

    c. I generally sleep long and soundly, and have difficulty waking up

24.

    a. I have lots of dreams but can't remember them specifically

    b. I can remember most of my dreams; I often dream in color

    c. I only remember dreams when they are intense or significant

Now add up the total of:

    a: _____   b: _____   c: _____

You will probably find that one of these numbers is highest. If you have mostly a's, then you are a Vata. If you have mostly b's, then you are a Pitta. If you have mostly c's, then you are a Kapha.

If two of the columns are equal, or very close, you may be a double-dosha. If that's the case, add up the number of a's, b's and c's in the Mind category and then the Body category to see where each dosha is dominant. This will give you more insight into your own situation as you read on.

Comparative totals for double-doshas:

MIND

    Vata (a)_____ Pitta (b)_____ Kapha (c)_____

BODY

    Vata (a)_____ Pitta (b)_____ Kapha (c)_____

RESULTS

Now you know whether you are predominantly Vata, Pitta, Kapha, or some combination of two. Whichever you are, be aware that aspects of the other, nondominant doshas will still come into play in certain situations. So keep your other scores in mind when reading through the chapters.

I will often refer to people who are Vata-, Pitta-, or Kapha-dominant as Vatas, Pittas, or Kaphas. The correct way to pluralize these words in Sanskrit is Vataja, Pittaja, and Kaphaja, but to make it easier for you to follow and understand, I've simply added an "s."

Once you have determined what your dosha is, you can use the same questions to figure out the doshas for your loved ones. You can then turn to the chapter on your particular love match (if you are Vata and your partner is Kapha, you would go to Chapter 5) and find out how to keep that relationship nurtured and in great shape.

Ayurveda helps us understand our natural tendencies, how we operate, and what it takes for us to get along with the people in our lives. Through learning about our doshas, we learn to recognize our strengths and work on our weaknesses.

Each chapter will give you insight into the individual doshas as well as how they work together. A quick-tempered Pitta woman, for example, may learn to be more patient with her even-keeled Kapha partner. Or a "big picture" Vata man may discover the benefits of being more detail-oriented with his Pitta mate.

Each of these chapters can apply to same-sex relationships too. Ayurveda considers the male and the female to be simply different types of energy, and any relationship is about the meeting of two energies. Whether it is a male/male relationship or a female/female relationship, it is each person's energy that dictates the dynamics of that relationship. In Chapter 14, we look at friendships among the dosha pairs, and aspects of this will apply as well.

As we grow in our knowledge, our connection with one another becomes more apparent and we become more aware of the impact that our relationships have on the world. We become more compassionate, more accepting, and more empathetic. May your exploration of these nine "love matches" and your own relationships bring you to a new depth of self-knowledge and help you manifest everything your heart desires.

BALANCE & BLISS:
YOUR NATURE, YOUR SELF

Listen to presences inside poems.
Let them take you where they will.
Follow those private hints,
and never leave the premises.
—RUMI

REGARDLESS OF WHAT'S going on with the people in your life, you need to remember that you also have a very important relationship with yourself! It really is up to you to keep your own mind and body healthy. When you are healthier, you are naturally happier, and vice versa. Our minds and bodies are intricately connected.

Ayurveda is most well-known as an alternative form of health care. Ayurvedic medicine originated in India, where it has been around for over 5,000 years. Because of the tremendous work and dedication of people like Dr. Deepak Chopra and Dr. Vasant Lad, Ayurveda has become widely recognized in the United States as a valuable system of healing. Today, many doctors combine Ayurveda and Western medicine in a harmonious blend of Eastern and Western wisdom.

The principle behind Ayurveda is balance. Ayurveda is used in two ways: as a preventive health-care system that seeks to keep the body balanced, and as a responsive health-care system to bring the body back into balance. While Western medicine looks at an illness and tries to rid the patient of his or her symptoms, Ayurveda looks at the whole patient and seeks to bring him or her back into a state of balance, thereby creating a natural state of health.

The mind-body balance is obtained through a connection between the mind and body, where thought acts on matter to create health or illness. In the place where mind meets body, there are three operating principles of nature, also known as doshas. Although we cannot see these doshas, we see the effect that they have on our minds and bodies. They operate as "metabolic principles." Each person is born with a unique combination of these three doshas, which make up his or her mind-body type. The goal is to find your particular mind-body type and keep it in balance for optimum health. This balance is achieved through diet, exercise, and lifestyle.

Health is more than the physical—it is also mental, emotional, and spiritual; Ayurveda therefore can be used to help us create and maintain healthy relationships. It can help us to better understand ourselves and the people in our lives. We can work with our natural strengths to help balance each other out. We can stop trying to "change" others to fit our needs and instead accept a person's characteristics as a part of his or her wholeness, and honor who they are.

The chart below shows the basic composition of Vata, Pitta, and Kapha. It is from these principles that all of the other characteristics are derived.

Ayurvedic Mind-Body Type Characteristics of the Three Doshas

	VATA	PITTA	KAPHA
Function:	Controls movement	Controls metabolism	Controls structure
Key word:	"Changeable"	"Intense"	"Relaxed"
Governs:	Colon	Intestines, stomach	Chest
Dominant senses:	Sound, touch	Sight	Taste, smell
Properties:	Cold, dry, light, rough	Hot, light, sharp, moist	Cold, heavy, wet, sticky
Composed of:	Air (& Space)	Fire (& Water)	(Water) & Earth

VATA

Vata-type people are generally thin and find it hard to gain weight. Because of this, Vatas have very little energy reserve and can tire easily and become unbalanced. Vatas need to get sufficient rest and not overdo things, stay warm, and stick to a regular routine.

The Vata dosha controls all movement in the body, including breathing, digestion, and nerve impulses from the brain. When Vata is out of balance, anxiety and other nervous disorders may be present. Digestive problems, constipation, cramps, and even premenstrual pain usually are attributed to a Vata imbalance.

The most important thing to know about Vata is that it leads the other doshas. Vata usually goes out of balance first, which causes the early stages of disease. More than half of all illnesses are Vata disorders. Balancing Vata is important for everyone, because when Vata is in balance, Pitta and Kapha are generally in balance, as well.

PITTA

Pitta-type people are generally of medium size and well-proportioned. They have a medium amount of physical energy and stamina. They also tend to be intelligent and have a sharp wit and a good ability to concentrate.

Fire is a characteristic of Pitta, whether it shows up as fiery red hair or a short temper. Because Pittas' body temperature is generally warm, Pitta types can go out of balance with overexposure to the sun. Their eyes are sensitive to light. They are ambitious by nature but also can be demanding and abrasive.

Pitta types are known for their strong digestion but should be careful not to abuse it. Their heat makes them particularly thirsty, and they should take caution not to douse their *agni,* or digestive fire, with too much liquid during meals.

Pitta dosha leads us to crave moderation and purity. We rely on Pitta to regulate our intake of food, water, and air. Any toxins, such as alcohol or tobacco, show up as a Pitta imbalance. Toxic emotions such as jealousy, intolerance, and hatred also should be avoided, to keep Pitta in balance for optimum health.

KAPHA

Kapha-type people tend to have sturdy, heavy frames that provide a good reserve of physical strength and stamina. This strength gives Kaphas a natural resistance to disease and a generally positive outlook about life.

The Kapha dosha is slow, and Kapha types tend to be slow eaters with slow digestion. They also speak slowly. They are calm and affectionate but, when out of balance, can become stubborn and lazy. They learn slowly, with a methodical approach, but also retain information well with a good understanding of it.

Kapha dosha controls the moist tissues of the body, so a Kapha imbalance may show up as a cold, allergies, or asthma. This is worse in Kapha season, March through June. Cold and wet weather aggravates Kapha.

Kapha types need to progress to stay in balance. They should not dwell in the past or resist change. They need lots of exercise and need to be careful not to overeat. Kaphas need stimulation to bring out their vitality. Kapha dosha teaches us steadiness and a sense of well-being.

HOW TO RECOGNIZE A DOSHA ON SIGHT

You'll notice that body types are genetic. In the same way, you'll often see one dosha dominant in a family. Each of us was born with our unique balance of doshas; with this knowledge, we can create for ourselves a lifestyle that keeps us healthy and happy. Here are some general characteristics to help you recognize someone's dosha at a first meeting.

	VATA	PITTA	KAPHA
Hair	dry	fine, usually straight; may be reddish, sandy, thinning, or prematurely gray	thick, oily, often dark and curly
Eyes	small, dark, often close set or wide set	bright; often gray or blue	large, wide, thick lashes and brows
Build	thin body frame, light muscles, long legs and arms	medium body frame, often muscular	solid, sturdy; large bones and muscles; may be overweight
Skin	dry, rough, thin; visible veins	warm, pale, ruddy; may have freckles	thick, oily, smooth, cool
Nails	brittle; may have ridges	medium in size, pinkish in color	large, smooth, white in color
Voice	low, weak, quick, talkative	high, sharp, clear, organized, argumentative	deep, slow, silent; good vocalists
Lips	thin, dry	medium in size, pinkish in color	full, moist
Walking pace	quick, uneven, hyper	moderate, goal-oriented	slow, steady

DOUBLE-DOSHAS

When you are a double-dosha, two doshas are presenting them-selves strongly in your constitution. This means that you can have obvious qualities of each of the two doshas. These qualities do not blend together but rather show their influence individually, in dif-ferent traits.

The first thing to do is to look at which dosha is dominant in both the mind and the body section (see quiz on page 4). You may be one dosha in mind and another in body. If this is the case, you can follow one routine when it comes to the physical and another when it comes to the mental issues. If you have both doshas in both areas, you need to use the remedies that are appropriate for that particular condition at the time.

VATA-PITTA

If Vata is dominant in the body, then you probably are thin like a Vata dosha-dominant person. You are also quick, humorous, and talkative, but since Pitta is present, you may be more ambitious than pure Vatas. Pitta lends some stability and strength but also may bring a tendency toward anger. You may have a stronger digestion because of Pitta's fire, which also improves circulation.

If Pitta is dominant in the body, you'll look more like the muscular Pitta type. Vata's influence may make you a little more prone to getting stressed out and nervous.

Read about both Vata and Pitta and see what parts apply more to your own situation.

PITTA-KAPHA

Kapha is so structurally strong that you will most likely have a heavier physique, even if Kapha is not dominant for you in the body section of the quiz. Pitta's influence makes you more muscular than pure Kapha types, though.

If Pitta is more dominant in the mind section, you will have more drive and ambition, but that may also mean you have more of a tendency toward anger and criticism.

If Kapha is more dominant in the mind section, you will be more laid-back but more prone to laziness. You need motivation to get active.

Read about both Pitta and Kapha and see what parts apply more to your own situation.

KAPHA-VATA

This is a pretty rare type because Kapha and Vata seem to be opposites in so many ways.

If Vata is dominant in the body section of the quiz, then you will most likely be thin like a Vata yet relaxed and laid-back like a

Kapha. You can be quick like a Vata, yet procrastinate like a Kapha. Both Kaphas and Vatas dislike the cold.

If Kapha is dominant in the body, you are more solidly built and may display Vata in your creativity and zest for life. Because of Vata's digestive sensitivity, watch your diet carefully.

Read about both Kapha and Vata and see what parts apply more to your own situation.

TRI-DOSHAS

When all of the scores are within one point of each other, or evenly distributed, you are one of the rare tri-doshas. When you are this mind-body type, you are more likely to remain in balance, because the ratio of Vata, Pitta, and Kapha is nearly even. You will tend to have lifelong good health and a good immune system. However, whenever you do get out of balance, you must work harder to balance all three doshas, because you don't have a "lead" dosha to start with.

If you're tri-doshic, it may be hard to figure out some of the answers to the questions in the quiz; your body type may be obscured by a Vata imbalance. Vata is the more dominant dosha and can often resemble Pitta or Kapha. For example, you may be small-boned but overweight. A Vata imbalance could very well cause such confusion.

The doshas like to move around, and there are hundreds of ways that they relate to each other, so to be a tri-dosha at birth is highly improbable. You may find, as you become more familiar with the doshas, that you're actually a double-dosha type after all. The most important thing to remember is not to try to fit yourself into a particular category, but to learn as much as you can about yourself. The tri-dosha needs to be more careful about keeping in balance with the seasons and the clock (pages 20–22 in this chapter) and seeing how each dosha expresses itself in the mind and body. Go back to the quiz on page 4 and figure out which dosha is dominant in the mind section and which dosha is more dominant in the body section.

DOSHA DIAGNOSIS

An Ayurvedic physician can provide you with the most accurate diagnosis of your mind-body type. Typically, the doctor will use a special pulse diagnosis, ask you to answer a series of questions, and look at your tongue and your physical features to determine your particular combination of doshas. The doctor can also detect any imbalances and recommend specific Ayurvedic herbs and lifestyle adjustments, if necessary. If you are interested in learning more about Ayurveda and adopting this lifestyle, particularly if you are not feeling well, it would be a good idea to consult with an Ayurvedic professional.

Vata, Pitta, and Kapha doshas are present in everyone, in different proportions. And all three doshas need to be kept in balance. Being in balance not only means being healthier and happier, but being the best person you can be! Here are some of the character traits of doshas when they are in balance versus when they are out of balance.

	VATA	PITTA	KAPHA
When in balance, you are	enthusiastic alert flexible creative talkative responsive	loving content intelligent articulate courageous	affectionate steady methodical high stamina resistant to illnesses
When out of balance, you are	restless fatigued constipated anxious underweight	perfectionistic frustrated angry impatient irritable prematurely gray or have early hair loss	dull prone to oily skin prone to allergies possessive prone to oversleeping overweight

REMEDIES AND ROUTINES

Your personal balance of the doshas will determine the proper Ayurvedic routine for your mind-body type. Here are some examples of dosha-balancing habits that you can use to start creating a routine that will help you function optimally.

	VATA	PITTA	KAPHA

Aggravated by (avoid)	wind
	caffeine
	traveling
	irregular routine
	irregular meals
	cold, dry weather
	excessive mental
	  work
		heat
		alcohol
		smoking
		pressure
		stress
		excessive spicy
		  or salty foods
		excessive activity
			cold
			damp
			oversleeping
			overeating
			heavy foods
			too little variety
			  in life

Pacified by (favor)	moisture warm, cooked foods good sleep habits regular mealtimes warm weather time to relax	cool weather cool foods, salads downtime cool bath or swim moonlight	warmth physical activity mental activity spontaneity spices

WHERE TO FIND THE DOSHAS

Once you know which dosha or doshas are dominant for you, you will be better able to decide which doshas are a better match for you in various relationships. In general, we want someone who will balance us out, rather than someone who will give us more of what we already have. So, if you're looking to meet someone with a particular dosha, where do you go? Where do they hang out? Here are a few ideas to get you thinking:

	VATA	PITTA	KAPHA
Favorite hobbies or things to do	travel culture comedy anything out of the ordinary	sports politics team or group competitions	water sports gardening business, finance

The doshas express themselves in every aspect of our lives. They are even active when we are asleep! Here are some ways that our doshas are apparent in the intimacy area of our relationships. I have included money here because while some people are free about sharing their bodies, it is difficult for them to share their check-books.

	VATA	PITTA	KAPHA
dreams	flying, falling	problem solving, test-taking	romantic, involving water
particularly sensitive to	music, sounds, touch	mood lighting	seductive scents, good food and drink
money-spending tendencies	usually spends too much money, often on unnecessary things	doesn't spend much money on day-to-day things, but splurges on luxuries	doesn't like spending money, has lots of money in savings

DOSHAS AND THE CALENDAR

Weather and seasonal changes affect our balance, and we can all benefit from adapting our routines to the seasons. November through February, when it is cold and dry, is Vata season. As windy, cold, and dry weather continues, Vata accumulates in the environment and can cause a Vata imbalance in the body. During this season, it is a good idea to adopt a more Vata diet and routine to keep Vata in balance. Stay warm, eat warm foods, and don't wear yourself out.

Pitta season comes during the summer, July through October, when the weather is hot. To keep Pitta in balance during this time, eat cool foods, such as salads. Drink cool (not ice-cold) liquids and avoid too much sun.

March through June is Kapha season, when it is cold and wet. It's during this time that you are more likely to get a cold from a Kapha imbalance. Stay warm, eat light meals, and get enough regular exercise to help keep Kapha in balance.

	VATA	PITTA	KAPHA
Season	November–February (cold and dry)	July–October (hot)	March–June (cold and wet)

DOSHAS AND THE CLOCK

Just as the seasons contain elements of the doshas, so do the hours of the day. At sunrise, or about 6:00 AM, the day's cycle begins with Kapha. To take advantage of the Kapha cycle, it is best to awaken between 6:00 AM and 8:00 AM. On awakening, you probably feel slow, relaxed, and calm—all Kapha attributes. Kapha time lasts until about 10:00 AM. Even young children can reap the benefits of the Kapha hours by getting up early.

From 10:00 AM to 2:00 PM, it is Pitta time. You are at your most active and efficient during these hours. At noon, or lunchtime, your appetite is at its peak. You should eat lunch between noon and 1:00 PM in order to use Pitta to your advantage. Lunch should also be your largest meal of the day. Parents should pack nutritious snacks and lunches for children that include the foods best suited for their particular mind-body type. This is the best time for children to take tests in school because it is their most productive learning time.

Vata time begins at 2:00 PM and lasts until 6:00 PM, and it's when you are most alert and creative. A light dinner should be eaten before 6:00 PM if possible, to take advantage of this energy.

The cycle repeats again in the evening hours. Kapha time is from 6:00 PM to 10:00 PM. Sunset brings to the body rest and a slower pace. It is best to go to bed by 10:00 PM to take advantage of the natural Kapha rhythm of this time. For optimal digestion, eat dinner at least three hours before bedtime. Younger children, who need more sleep should go to bed earlier so that they can still wake at sunrise.

Pitta time is 10:00 PM to 2:00 AM, when Pitta keeps the body warm; the body also uses the Pitta heat to digest food and rebuild body tissues.

Vata time occurs again at 2:00 AM to 6:00 AM. Vata creativity is expressed in the form of active dreams. At this time, brain impulses are at their most active for the night.

THE AYURVEDIC DAILY CLOCK

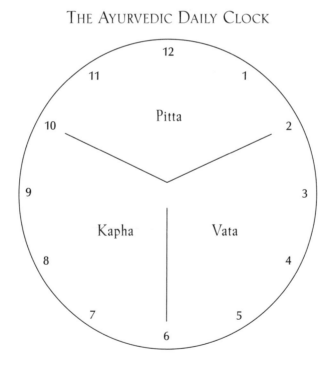

3

VATA WOMAN
&
VATA MAN

When I am with you, we stay up all night.
When you're not here, I can't go to sleep.
Praise God for these two insomnias!
And the difference between them.
—RUMI

ATTRACTION

WHEN PEOPLE OF the same mind-body type are attracted to each other, they usually see themselves in one another. They mirror each other, whether it is physically, mentally, or both. It's a kind of "simpatico" relationship.

With Vatas, it's like looking at a pair of birch trees. The air and space that composes this dosha swirls around them poetically.

Vatas are drawn to each other because they understand each other. Others may see them as spacey or restless, but Vatas recognize their own innate creativity, their need to express themselves. Vatas tend to think very quickly, and it is a pleasure for them to meet someone who responds at the same pace.

Because Vatas are so moved by the arts, they often encounter other Vatas in their social circle. This is often another quality that attracts Vatas to each other—a common love of music, art, or philosophy. Vatas are passionate about creativity and that passion is easily transferred to one who is creative.

Bliss

One reason a Vata–Vata match works is because this pair shares not only many common interests, but often a similar sense of humor.

LIFESTYLE

Vists a Vata household and you'll most likely find a warm and cozy atmosphere. Vatas have an aversion to the cold and prefer to stay indoors, away from the wind. There will be a fire in the fireplace and the Vata lovebirds will be wearing each other's clothes, usually comfy sweatshirts and wool socks.

One of the key attributes of the Vata dosha is variability. Because their appetites, sleep patterns, digestion, and energy levels are so variable, Vatas are best together when they are in sync with each other's rhythms. A ravenously hungry Vata man will be disheartened when his Vata companion just nibbles at the feast that he has prepared for her. He'll understand, but because his Vata mind works overtime, he'll worry that she doesn't like something about the meal. After he's overeaten and is feeling bloated, the compassionate Vata gal will empathize and soothe his tummy with gentle strokes, and all will be well in Vataville once again.

Because too much Vata leads to imbalance, it is important that the Vatas work together to keep their Vata in check. They can help each other do this by keeping regular hours, eating warm, cooked foods, and spending time near the water.

One of the best exercises for balancing Vata is dancing, and Vata mates make lovely partners! Vatas respond so well to music that there is an additional benefit there. When the music is soft and sweet and their two bodies touch and share warmth, the Vata couple glides gracefully across the floor. Fred Astaire and Ginger

Rogers are an excellent example of the artistic possibilities when two Vatas get together. If the Vata girl can get her guy to a yoga class, he'll find the exercise another great way to keep in balance and spend time with his beloved. Another wonderful routine for these two would be a daily walk, to shake off the stress of the workday and help stimulate the appetite before their evening meal.

A Word of Advice

The most important thing that the Vata–Vata couple can do to keep their doshas in balance is to maintain a regular routine. Wake up and go to sleep at the same times each day; eat meals at the same times each day.

COMMUNICATION

Vatas are very talkative, so when you get two of them together, it's hard to get a word in edgewise! It's kind of funny listening to Vatas talking to each other, especially when they know each other well. They're always finishing each other's sentences and interrupting each other because they already know what the other one is going to say.

Because Vatas think and talk so quickly, it is important that the Vata couple watch out for misunderstandings and miscommunications. Especially when enthusiasm is high, as it often is with Vatas, it can be a big letdown to find that you were each really talking about two entirely different things.

Often, Vatas are a lot of talk and very little action. They may flit from one idea to another, starting lots of new projects with good intentions but little or no follow-through. In order for the Vata couple to get anything accomplished, it is often necessary for them to have a written-out plan where each task is defined. That way, the two can stay on track. Vatas tend to think in terms of the "big picture," but if they take the time to piece out each project they can achieve their mutual goals more reasonably. Vatas have a fairly poor long-term memory, so a written account is a useful tool in any circumstance.

EMOTIONS

Because Vatas are so quick, sometimes they speak before they think. So although they are very sensitive people, they can appear insensitive and inadvertently hurt someone's feelings with a hasty remark. Put two Vatas together and you get a lot of that. But at least it works both ways, and if the couple understands the pure intentions behind the words, they can work on these bad habits together and forgive each other when need be.

When out of balance, Vatas can be extremely nervous and anxiety-ridden. Unfortunately, that kind of thing is easy for another sensitive Vata to pick up on, and those bad vibes can feed off on each other and multiply. When this happens, Vatas can help each other by invoking calming and warming Vata-reducing techniques.

To keep emotions in check, it is essential for Vatas to meditate on a regular basis. When two or more people meditate together, it increases the energy in the room and benefits everyone there. Vatas need this calming, centering influence in their lives to handle all the little annoying things that usually set them off.

Vatas get worried easily; a Vata couple will need to spend time reassuring one another so that the worry doesn't escalate. It is great for Vatas to express their emotions creatively—this is very freeing for them and helps to keep them in touch with their feelings without letting those feelings get out of control. And when they team up, anything is possible, so it's best to strive for the positive. For example, one Vata might write a beautiful poem, and his or her Vata partner may then set it to music. Another Vata team might create and decorate a cake reminiscent of the Taj Mahal. Life is like one big piece of performance art to the most creative Vata types.

Challenges

Because these two are so similar in temperament, each must be careful not to exacerbate the other's negative qualities. They can send each other into a tailspin of nervousness and anxiety!

SEX

Vatas are all about romance, so these two will woo each other all day, every day. They love the build-up and will sustain it as long as possible. Vatas love to fantasize and let their creativity run wild, so they will happily indulge in games and role-playing. You might even find a little trunk of costumes and props hidden somewhere in the Vata bedroom.

As in other areas, the Vata's interest will be variable when it comes to sex. If their attention and enthusiasm is focused elsewhere, sex is not a priority. Both Vata men and women are easily distracted. But when a Vata is passionate, that passion is intense!

Vatas love to be touched, and touch is so soothing and balancing for this dosha. The two can spend hours just stroking and cuddling, wrapped in the warmth of each other's arms. Vatas communicate volumes through touch.

In terms of fertility, pure Vata types rate pretty low. These couples tend to have fewer children than other combinations. It helps to become more Kapha-like when trying to conceive: Slow down, mellow out, and eat regularly.

FOOD

Of the three mind-body types, Vatas are the pickiest eaters. This is probably because their digestion is very delicate. Vata governs the colon and when out of balance, Vatas are prone to irritable bowel syndrome. Since Vata is composed of air and space, it is easy for

Vatas to get gas. With all these things going on, Vatas need to watch what they eat.

The Vata appetite, like everything else about this dosha, is variable. Many of those tall thin supermodels (who say that they can eat everything in sight and not gain an ounce) are Vata types. They may gorge themselves at an all-you-can-eat pasta bar, or be content with a breadstick and soda water.

To keep Vata in balance, this couple needs to keep a regular routine when it comes to meals. Even if one of them doesn't feel like eating a lot, they should each eat something at regular intervals. Vatas like to snack, but then they don't get the nourishment that they really need from their food. It's best to establish good eating habits, to promote proper healthy digestion.

The Basic Rules for the Vata Diet

Food should be warm and cooked, rather than raw.

Favor tastes that are sweet, sour, and salty.

Avoid eating cold, dry foods, like chips or crackers, or add a warm dipping sauce to accompany these foods.

Avoid caffeine. Caffeine aggravates Vata and causes imbalance.

For example, a Vata breakfast might be oatmeal, rather than cold cereal, sweetened with some brown sugar and soy milk. Many Vatas are lactose-intolerant, so soy milk is a nice alternative. Caffeine is particularly aggravating to Vata, so instead of regular coffee, serve herbal tea or decaffeinated coffee. Coffee substitutes are often better than coffee because of coffee's acid content, which may disturb Vata's digestion.

Because Vatas have such a dilemma with their diets, and because they are such creative people, many Vatas love to cook their own meals. The only problem is that sometimes they'll taste-test recipes so much that they're not hungry once the meal is prepared! The Vata couple can have a lot of fun together in the kitchen, creating wonderful delicacies that they both will enjoy.

TRAVEL

Vata is aggravated by travel, so Vata people have a difficult time traveling. It's a combination of the strange, unusual food; the excessive movement necessary to get anywhere; and the nervousness and anxiety that come from the whole experience. Ginger tea is a good remedy to help bring Vata back into balance when traveling. Vatas get carsick, airsick, and motionsick, so it's no surprise that many Vatas are homebodies and prefer not to travel at all.

On the other hand, Vatas love new and different experiences. They love interesting, unusual places, and they love to stimulate their minds and their senses. Once Vatas manage to get wherever they're going to go, they love being there. But it is important to make sure they have enough time to transition their bodies to the new climate and/or time zone so that they are comfortable and can function. The process of traveling is difficult for this Vata team, but the actual vacationing is wonderful.

The Vata couple enjoy themselves most on a trip where their activities are varied. They'll want a few days just to veg out and relax. They'll also want a few days to explore the environment. Vatas love to shop, so that should be included on the agenda. And, of course, they'll want to decide what to do spontaneously, depending on how they feel that particular day!

Climate-wise, the Vatas prefer warm weather. It's best to stay away from dry places, like the desert, which will aggravate Vata. Any place that has a lot of sunshine and is near the water, which provides a little humidity, is ideal for this pair. A tropical island is heaven on earth for Vatas!

Getaway

Vatas love any place that is warm and humid. Hawaii, Florida, Tahiti, the Bahamas . . . even a steam room can be a sexy getaway for these two!

WORK

Vatas like to be active and their restless nature makes it hard for them to sit behind a desk all day. They also have a deep need to express their creativity, and they make wonderful musicians, artists, teachers, and philosophers. Vatas are highly intelligent and like to banter with others. This couple will never run out of things to say to each other!

Vatas work quickly, and they have a low tolerance level for those who can't keep up with them. That is one reason the Vatas, when paired together, respect one another so much. They have little patience for anyone who doesn't "get it" as fast as they do.

It's fun to have Vatas around in a work environment. As long as their strengths are utilized, Vatas can be an asset on the job. Many Vatas run successful businesses on their own. But Vatas are not great when it comes to managing money; it's best if they hire someone who is good at handling the details so that the taxes get filed on time and the bills get paid.

Because this couple put so much of themselves into their work, it is easy for them to get burned out. They literally use themselves up and end up depleted of energy. Rather than let things get to this point, the Vata duo should strive for balance and encourage each other to rest up and conserve some of their precious energy for other endeavors.

Business

The Vata–Vata couple will succeed in a business where they both enjoy what they are doing, and this probably means something in the arts. They could open a gallery, write screenplays together, or run their own dinner theater.

GREAT DATES

Dinner and a movie are not going to impress a Vata—unless it's dinner at an exotic Mongolian restaurant and a well-reviewed but little-known foreign film afterward. Vatas like things out of the ordinary. These two like spontaneity, but if they leave plans up in the air all the time they may get frustrated with each other when things don't work out. It's best if they take turns with the arrangements and surprise each other with fun things to do when they go out.

The Vata couple would have a good time at a comedy club or a modern art museum. They might like to spend the weekend redecorating their apartments and shopping for unusual accessories to finish off the funky new look. Vatas are very sensitive to sound, so they should stay away from noisy places and crowds.

SENSUAL PLEASURES

It's all about touch for the Vata couple. They can't get enough of it. It starts with hand-holding and winds up as a full-body massage. The hands are channels for energy to flow through, and both the Vata man and Vata woman are particularly sensitive to these vibrations.

Music is mellowing for Vatas. They tend to like slow jazz or music with an exotic flavor. This can be playing softly in the background when a seduction is to take place.

The biggest turnoff for Vatas is if the room is too cold. Vatas need warmth; it's a good idea for them to build a fire or snuggle under blankets to be comfortable. A warm drink, such as sake, brandy, or hot chocolate spiked with almond liqueur or frothy with marshmallows, helps Vata to relax and maybe even melt.

AT HOME

The Vata home is filled with artwork on the walls and on every countertop. Some of the art is purchased, but much of it is created by one or both of the partners. There are usually stacks of papers around, unfinished projects, half-read books, magazines with torn-out pages for ideas and inspiration.

Sinces Vatas are always on the go, busy experiencing all that can be experienced in the big world out there, their homes are often empty. But at night they find their way home and get comfy under their down comforter before drifting off to dreamland.

It is a good idea for Vatas to decorate their home with warm, soothing colors. They tend to like splashy colors and bright prints, but these only stimulate Vata more, which is the last thing this couple needs. Vatas require a calming environment; one way to do that is to keep clutter to a minimum. A calm mind will bring about a relaxed body, which will make Vata much more efficient and happy.

In the kitchen, these two must stay stocked with lots of whole-some foods that they can simply heat up or microwave. Vatas are busy people and they will gravitate toward the snack cupboard if left to their own devices.

CIRCLE OF FRIENDS

Vatas can be loners—so when they're a couple, they can isolate themselves in their own little Vata world. Vatas also make friends easily, so it's good for them to get out and socialize—it makes them happy, especially when they're telling stories to an audience who is hanging on their every word. The Vatas seem like party people, but what you don't see is that it's hard for them to get there. They have fun once they're at the party, but beforehand they go through a lot of anxiety trying to figure out what to wear, what to bring, and when to arrive.

Vatas love to surround themselves with creative people; you'll often find them congregating at a late-night dinner after the theater, or sipping cocktails at a gallery opening.

Family Dynamics

Since mind-body types are genetic, there are likely strong Vata types on both sides of the Vata couple's families. So things like worry, which easily can become a habit, are inherited. By keeping their Vata in balance, this couple can avoid some of the anxiety that they are so familiar with. The upside is that things like creativity and a great sense of humor are also inherited, and these will go a long way toward creating a strong and healthy family environment in which they can thrive.

As parents, the Vatas need to remember how much they value self-expression, and keep it in mind when their children go off into their own little Vata spins. They also need to teach their children calmness and restraint, and the best way to do this is by example. The children can be creative and expressive, but that doesn't mean they should be allowed to draw on the walls!

4

VATA WOMAN
&
PITTA MAN

My sweetheart
You have aroused my passion
Your touch has filled me with desire
I am no longer separate from you.
—RUMI

ATTRACTION

THE VATA WOMAN–Pitta man combination is combustible! They look beautiful together, and people can tell from the energy generated by these two that love is in the air.

He is attracted to her sinewy frame, her feminine movements, and her come-hither smile. She is attracted to his muscular shoulders, his sparkling eyes, and his warm touch. He likes her enthusiasm and style. She likes his intellect and is impressed with his rapid recall.

If there is some past-life connection, some glimmer of recognition, it could be love at first sight for these two. The attraction is that instantaneous. Her air fans his flame, and their love can burn brightly for many lifetimes.

If they can each manage to stay in balance, then their relationship will actually be as idyllic as it looks to be from the outside. Of course, balance takes some effort, but a strong attraction is a great motivator and these two certainly have that going for them!

Bliss

The Vata–Pitta couple has a lot of fun together. They enjoy each other's company and are content whether they are stuck in traffic or indulging in a candlelight dinner. As long as they have each other, that's all they need!

LIFESTYLE

The Pitta man can be very loving and give his Vata partner all the attention she craves. He's happiest when he's busy, and she definitely has enough going on in her life to keep him interested. But because excessive activity throws him out of balance, and excessive mental activity throws her out of balance, these two need to make sure they spend lots of downtime at home just doing nothing, and preferably doing it together.

There will be a lot of negotiation in this household. First there is the thermostat to consider. She likes the room to be warm and he likes it cool. But both are willing to compromise to please the other. She might put on a sweater while he peels down to a tank top; she's happy to have those rippling muscles of his in full view, anyway!

There's also the matter of sleeping arrangements. Her side of the bed will be loaded with thick blankets, while most nights he's happy with just a sheet. She's not a restful sleeper; she's generally up a few times in the night. But he sleeps soundly and is unaware of her movements for the most part.

The Pitta man loves to compete, but the Vata woman is not a challenge for him when it comes to sports. He'll have to get out there with his buddies and play. She's content to cheer for her man from the sidelines. Swimming is a great exercise for the Pitta man, but unless the pool is heated, you won't catch his Vata lady anywhere near it. But it doesn't matter; there are plenty of indoor sports they can enjoy together.

COMMUNICATION

The Vata woman talks fast and is never at a loss for words, but she'll find herself having to repeat herself when she has conversations with her Pitta man. The Pitta man is extremely discerning, and he needs to have clear in his mind exactly what is going on. He'll ask lots of questions of her and sometimes she'll lose her train of thought.

If these two can understand their communication styles, they can adapt them to suit each other. Either he waits until she is finished and then asks questions, or she moderates her pace and offers more detail because she knows that's what he is looking for. Patience in matters of communication will pay off several times over for both of them.

When the Pitta man communicates, he can often come off as blunt or cold. He is very articulate and chooses his words wisely. He has been accused of being too "logical" in his demeanor. But what he's really trying to do is to make sure he is understood. He can be forceful about presenting his ideas and feelings, but that is only because they are so important to him. His beliefs are strong, and that comes across in the way he speaks. His Vata lady is very sensitive and may find his approach to be abrupt. The Pitta man needs to be aware of this and try to be gentler with her. And she needs to understand that this is just the way he is and not take it to heart.

The Vata woman learns things very quickly and then she forgets them just as fast. The Pitta man has a much better memory and he'll remember the things that his partner said. The Pitta male likes to be right; he'll often take notes so that if his recall fails, he can look something up. Ms. Vata can learn from her mate's good habits.

A Word of Advice

It is important for this couple to communicate clearly with one another. Because of their different communication styles, they may find that they are talking about two completely different things—then confusion and mayhem ensues!

EMOTIONS

As logical and analytical as the Pitta man tries to be, when out of balance, he can be aggressive and judgmental. He has a bad temper and can get very angry. It's important for his Vata lady to realize that this is his temperament and not to take it personally when he gets into one of his moods. This is often difficult for the sensitive Vata, who tends to personalize everything.

To cool him off, the savvy Vata girl will work to ease his stress by serving him a cool drink, preferably something fruity and sweet. Pittas should avoid alcohol because it will just aggravate their irritability. Ms. Vata can feed him strawberries and coo over him until Mr. Pitta forgets what he was upset about and remembers how lucky he is to be so well cared for.

The Vata woman is more moody than others are. She's a bundle of nervous energy and she wears her heart on her sleeve. Her moods are unpredictable. She is super-sensitive, so much depends on what is happening in her environment. When out of balance, she can be extremely anxious.

To calm his lady's fears, the smart Pitta male will speak in soothing tones. He'll tell her how wonderful she is, and how perfect their life is together. He'll stroke her hair and hold her close. When Vata feels loved, all is right with the world.

Challenges

The Pitta man must learn to overlook some of what he perceives as his Vata lady's "spaciness." In turn, the Vata in this relationship must learn to be patient with what she sees as her Pitta-honey's obsession with detail and organization. They both can learn from each other!

SEX

Since Pitta runs hot, it's no surprise that the Pitta male is pretty much ready to go anytime, anywhere. It doesn't take much to get this man aroused. He enjoys sex and considers it a form of communication with his beloved.

The Vata female has a variable level of interest in sex. She's more into romance. The Pitta male who understands this will be blissfully rewarded. With Vata, sex begins with engaging the heart and the mind. She's into fantasy and wants the candlelight and violins. But don't do the same thing every time or this girl will get bored! As long as she feels safe and comfortable, she likes to try new things and be surprised. When Vata passion is ignited with Pitta fire, the results are explosive!

Vata can be fragile at times, and she is most vulnerable when she is pregnant. A pregnant Vata needs even more attention than she usually does. Her Pitta partner can help get her through the awkward nine months by making sure she gets the proper nutrition and exercise. The Vata woman is prone to morning sickness, which causes her anxiety and throws her out of balance.

During this time, it's best for her loved one to help keep her Vata mind calm and focused on happy things. He can play her favorite soft music and massage her feet. The Pitta male likes to have a plan and needs to feel that he has an integral role in the process, and this is a good way to do that.

FOOD

The Vata and Pitta diets are almost opposite. She needs to have warm, cooked foods, and he does better on raw, cool foods. But there are plenty of areas where they can come together.

Salads are great for him, but he needs some protein with it to fill him up and fuel that Pitta stamina. Both Pitta and Vata do better with fish and poultry than red meat. Tofu and soy products are great alternatives that benefit them, as well. Avocados are balancing for both Vata and Pitta, so they should be included in meals whenever possible. Raw tomatoes and peppers are aggravating to Vata and Pitta, so make sure to leave those out.

Rice is a good balancing food for both Vata and Pitta. There are many Asian dishes that these two will readily agree on for dinner. The setting of a Thai restaurant is exotic and warming to the Vata girl and the spices and coconut in many of the meals are cooling to her Pitta guy.

TRAVEL

Travel is interesting for these two because they can have such different styles. The Pitta man loves to plan and has almost as much fun charting the course as he does making the journey. The Vata woman prefers to be more spontaneous and allow herself to "go with the flow." She's happy to let him make all the arrangements, as long as she can change them if she feels like doing something else! Fortunately, Mr. Pitta is adaptable and can work around his lady's whims. He's also compassionate and will do whatever is necessary to help her to feel comfortable in unfamiliar surroundings.

Ms. Vata will always want to go somewhere warm, and Mr. Pitta prefers cooler environments. So if they choose a warm area with a nice hotel that has air conditioning and a pool, they should both be happy!

Getaway

All this couple need is a moonlight walk on the beach. The sound of the ocean, which is so soothing to Vata, and the light of the moon, which does wonders for Pitta, is a magical combination for this pair.

WORK

The Pitta man is ambitious and the Vata woman likes that about him. He has a keen mind and knows how to work his way up in the world. Career is important to him; it brings him joy to see the fruits of his labor. At times, though, the driven Pitta can become a workaholic. He needs more balance in his life, and that's where his Vata companion can be so helpful.

The Vata woman is as creative as her Pitta cohort is ambitious. Where Pitta is the businessperson, Vata is the artist. These two make a remarkable team when they choose to work together. She will paint the big picture, and he can plot out the details.

Of the two, it is best to let Mr. Pitta handle the finances. Ms. Vata tends to overspend. He can keep track and account for expenses and the like in his precise manner; she just tosses receipts in a drawer and forgets about them. Although he is a moderate spender, he does love his luxuries, which suits his Vata lover splendidly. He may deduct their business lunches, but he'll treat her to something decadent when the occasion warrants.

Business

The Vata–Pitta couple would excel in public relations, marketing, or advertising. Businesses like these involve both creativity and strong people skills, which these two have in spades!

GREAT DATES

The Pitta man likes to have a plan for his dates and he's very good about taking care of all the details. He'll make reservations ahead of time, take the quickest route to the restaurant, and make sure the meal is complete in plenty of time to get to the 8:00 PM show. All this pleases Ms. Vata, who can simply relax and go along for the ride. She'll notice that he's washed his car (he generally keeps it immaculate) and will be impressed with his extensive CD collection as they cruise along together. All this organization is Mr. Pitta's version of romance. He's not a hearts and flowers kind of a guy, not sentimental at all.

If the Vata gal wants to plan something special for her Pitta guy, she may take him on a boat trip. Pittas love to be near the water; it is very cooling and balancing for them. They may go rowing (he can show off his rippling muscles) or on a gondola ride, where they can glide along peacefully and kiss under the bridges for luck.

SENSUAL PLEASURES

Mr. Pitta notices everything. He loves it when his lady dresses up or puts on something slinky just for him. He's a visual kind of guy—so if Vata wants to make her message loud and clear, all she needs to do is to get naked.

Pitta men get turned on by watching. So Ms. Vata can belly dance for him, or "accidentally" slip a steamy video into the VCR on a quiet night at home.

To seduce his Vata lady, Mr. Pitta needs to take it nice and slow. He needs to remember that while his fire is constantly roaring, hers may need some coaxing to ignite. The best thing he can do is to rub his warm hands all over her cool body and brush his lips softly over her skin. When he whispers sweet nothings in her ear, she just melts; she loves hearing him speak her name. What Pitta lacks in romance, he makes up for in passion, and Ms. Vata enjoys her time in bed with him.

At Home

The big conflict in this household is over the temperature. He wants to blast the air conditioner and she wants to turn up the heat. There are solutions to this! First of all, these two need to set up areas in the house where they can each have their own separate space, complete with climate control. He can get a portable fan and she a small electric heater. Those areas can be seen as retreats to warm up or cool off. In the areas that they share, Ms. Vata can bundle up in socks and a sweater while Mr. Pitta can run around barefoot in his tank top and shorts. In bed, she'll want an electric blanket and he'll just toss off his side of it and sleep under a sheet.

It's nice for this couple to have an aquarium in their home. The water is balancing for Pitta and the fish are calming for Vata. Pitta can take care of the pH balances and all that, and Vata can decorate this fantasy environment to her heart's content.

It's fun for these two to work on home projects together. They are particularly good at building or remodeling homes—he is a good engineer and she is creative with design. Once they settle into their own abode they may consider taking this partnership to another level by investing in properties that they can work on together.

Circle of Friends

Mr. Pitta makes lots of friends at work, so he'll be eager for his Vata lady to meet his posse at their various business functions. Ms. Vata will get her man to accompany her to her theater galas and charity events. They make quite a striking couple and are happy to show each other off in public.

It's great when this couple can mix it up with other Vata–Pitta couples. The Pittas can debate issues and compete at sports while the Vatas can compare notes on independent film festivals and awards.

This couple throws wonderful parties! Ms. Vata certainly knows how to entertain, and she knows how to keep the atmosphere lively for her enamored guests. Mr. Pitta has plenty of cool drinks on hand and is happy to take the lead as the congenial host.

FAMILY DYNAMICS

When it comes to parenting, the Pitta father is the disciplinarian in the family. He's very disciplined himself and instills those values in his children. Mr. Pitta is a smart guy and expects his children to study and do well in school. The Vata mother sees this as a strength in her hubby and allows him to use his influence in these areas. She is then free to help her children explore the more bohemian parts of the equation. She shows them how to have fun, how to cut loose, and how to appreciate the beauty of living in the moment.

When the kids are out late, the Vata mom is the first to worry. She makes up crazy scenarios in her head and doesn't rest until her children are safe at home in their beds. Hopefully, the kids have learned well enough to come home before the Pitta dad gets angry, so they can avoid one of his stern lectures on responsibility.

Many sitcom couples are made up of the Vata woman and the Pitta man. Lucy and Ricky and Dharma and Greg are just two examples.

5

Vata Woman & Kapha Man

I can sense your presence
in my heart
although you belong
to all the world.
—RUMI

Attraction

THE VATA WOMAN sees the Kapha man as the strong and dependable man who will take care of her forever. The Kapha man sees the Vata woman as a fragile treasure that needs looking after. As romance unfolds, they easily fall into these roles, he the rescuer, and she the fair maiden. His large eyes and thick lashes mesmerize her. Her delicate gestures captivate him. She feels safe in his arms. He feels protective and responsible for her.

When these two sustain these feelings, the attraction remains. Yet with Vata as variable as she is, she often grows restless. The Kapha man will see her as a free spirit and flighty with her affections. The Vata woman begins to see the Kapha man as boring, instead of stable. This couple can be good for each other if they use their good qualities to help balance each other out. But if they grow apart and the spell is broken, it is difficult to bring them back together.

Bliss

The Kapha man is at his best when he is stimulated, and the Vata woman is a firecracker! And when she gets a little too stressed, Mr. Kapha has a calming influence on his partner.

LIFESTYLE

Kapha needs to be stimulated to stay in balance, and the Vata woman provides stimulation in abundance! He never knows what she is going to do or say next. He never knows what she is going to get him to do next! Vata is definitely the protagonist in this relationship. She keeps things moving, and that is good for Kapha.

The flip side is that Kapha needs to work extra hard to keep his Vata lady interested. Once she tires of his routine, she'll tire of him. Vata likes change, but Kapha craves stability. It's as if Vata is a boat, and the Kapha man is her anchor. She can zip around and explore, but he keeps her from getting lost. But if Vata strays too far, or for too long a time, Kapha may just decide to let her go. He wants company at home, not out in the unfamiliar waters.

Because Kapha embraces stability, the couple is likely to live at the same address for many years. So for Vata to experience the change that she needs, she'll often rearrange the furniture or redecorate the house. Kapha will come home and roll his eyes, but pretty soon he'll come to expect a surprise every so often and understand that this is just one way for his Vata companion to express her creativity.

The Vata girl may seem hyperactive next to her laid-back Kapha guy. But this is a good thing. She needs to be calmer; he needs to be more active. If she can be patient with him and slow down a little bit, and he can perk up and try to keep up with her, there will be harmony in the household.

Challenges

Ms. Vata thrives on change; she'll stir things up if she gets bored. Mr. Kapha prefers stability and structure, which his partner might perceive as ho-hum.

COMMUNICATION

There is not a lot of disagreement with the Kapha man and Vata woman. Usually she can bat her eyes and he will give in to her wishes. But there is often miscommunication between these two, given their diametrically opposed styles. She talks fast, gets her point across quickly, and makes decisions spontaneously. He talks slowly, often repeating himself several times to make his point, and needs lots of time to mull things over before making a decision. They, of course, drive each other crazy over this. It helps greatly to be aware of these tendencies and allow the other person space to be true to his or her nature.

He thinks she's spacey, a bit of an airhead. She thinks he's stubborn, too set in his ways. She grows impatient with him, he digs in his heels, she gets frustrated, he yells, she cries, he caves, and she wins, again.

And then they make up. Vata is happy to have her dragon-slayer back by her side. Kapha is happy to be of service to this fiercely independent maiden.

Kapha men prefer to avoid conflict, so when something comes up that might be a little "sticky," it's usually up to Ms. Vata to solve it. She's not crazy about conflict herself, but is usually good at getting things done quickly and gracefully.

EMOTIONS

The Vata woman lives in a state of nervousness and anxiety and it is pretty much up to her calm Kapha man to create some balance in the household. Granted, his calm could be interpreted as laziness, when he is out of balance. He is content to lie on the couch for hours, while his Vata lady can't sit still for more than two minutes. She'll flit around putting things away or working on one of her many unfinished projects, while he watches TV or reads a book. This can lead to a great deal of time spent alone, so it would be best if this couple could find activities that they enjoy doing together.

The Kapha man may be easygoing, but he is also very possessive. He is territorial about his home and his Vata mate. He is very attached to his things and to his way of life, and when this is disturbed in any way, he can easily become depressed. Ms. Vata can help him feel secure by cooking his favorite meal—usually one of his mother's recipes from his childhood.

The Vata woman needs constant reassurance and this comes readily from the Kapha man. He is very caring and nurturing, an emotional rock for her. She, in turn, stimulates his emotions. He feels things more deeply when he is with her because she opens him up to new experiences and challenges.

A Word of Advice

With these two, it's hard to compromise sometimes; they need to work at learning how to "take turns."

SEX

In bed, the challenge for the Vata woman is to keep her Kapha man awake. He loves to sleep, and sleeps long and soundly. Because Vata's sexual appetite is variable, she may be content to let him do just that. But this is not a good way to maintain a relationship. Kapha needs stimulation. Vata needs to feel cared for. The two need to come up with something that will keep them both satisfied.

Kapha men tend to have a lot of stamina. They're slow to arouse but can maintain their passion for a long time. Depending on the Vata woman's current state of mind, this may be totally fascinating or downright dull.

To please his lady, Mr. Kapha needs to do more than merely last; he must indulge her fantasies, play along with her games. He's good at pouring on the romance, which gets Ms. Vata interested. If he can be sensitive to her moods and pick up on her nuances, they'll both have a good time.

FOOD

The Kapha man loves food and loves to eat. His appetite is always good, but if the food is tasty, he'll eat it even if he's not hungry. It's very easy for Mr. Kapha to overindulge. Food is his biggest weakness, and he is most likely to become overweight. Because Kapha is heavy, he can skip meals without a problem, but he rarely ever does.

The Vata woman, on the other hand, often has to be reminded to eat. She's so busy that mealtimes are often an inconvenience for her. But she desperately needs to get food on a regular basis as she has no real reserve of energy on her slight frame.

Both Kapha and Vata do better on warm, cooked foods. But other than that, the two diets have very little in common. Kapha is heavy, so Kapha men should favor lighter foods, avoiding oils and fried dishes. The Kapha man tends to have a sweet tooth, but this is his downfall. He should avoid desserts and high-fat sweets at all costs! When he sticks to a Kapha diet and gets enough exercise, the Kapha man will stay in balance and keep the weight off.

Ms. Vata may have a sweet tooth, but it doesn't show! It's okay if she partakes in some little luxuries. She prefers to nibble, so there's not much chance that she'll overdo.

Kaphas need stimulation in all areas of their lives, including their diet. They can get this with lots of different spices, chutneys, and sauces. Vatas are sensitive to spice and prefer more simply cooked fare.

The Vata woman may go through stages where she's involved in cuisine and embraces the kitchen, but usually she's so busy that she can't be bothered with cooking. This gives her Kapha man free rein at the stove, and he likes it that way! She likes it, too; it's another way that he can help take care of her.

TRAVEL

Even though Mr. Kapha prefers to stay at home, travel is very stimulating and thus very beneficial for him. It makes him feel energized, more alive and happy. He doesn't seem to be bothered by the time changes or the climate differences; all of these things just help to ignite his engine.

When these two are on a trip together, it once again falls to the Kapha man to take care of his Vata woman. During the plane ride, she'll be up and down several times visiting the restroom, so he'd better let her sit in the aisle seat. She'd also need to stay hydrated, since the dry air aggravates Vata terribly. He can help make sure she has water available at all times. And she'll also need to keep her mind on other things. Plane rides can get awfully boring, and this is torture for the Vata girl. With too much time on her hands, there's no limit to the possible scenarios she can dream up in her creative, anxious mind.

So, where to go? Both the Kapha man and Vata woman prefer warmer climates, but she can't take the dry and he can't take the damp. It's best to find somewhere with mild weather where they can spend lots of time just hanging out. He'll want to relax and she'll want to recover. Make sure there are plenty of shopping opportunities; he can give her his credit card and they'll both be happy—he'll get some quiet time for himself and she'll get to go out and circulate.

Getaway

Go sightseeing together. Kapha can walk around and experience new things, and Vata can shop and explore.

WORK

Chances are that the Vata woman will have several different jobs during the course of her career, possibly even in several different fields. It's also likely that the Vata woman will hold more than one job at a time. She's great at freelancing and consulting, and this keeps her interested by making each day different rather than routine.

The Vata woman is a lot better at dealing with people than she is at dealing with money. She tends to spend her money just as fast as she makes it. She's not really good at saving, so this is where her Kapha man can really help out.

The Kapha man is great at saving, maybe even too much so. He is extremely prudent and might even be called a tightwad. But Kapha is a good provider and is able to maintain a hefty savings account and contribute to his IRA. Because of his adeptness with all things financial, Mr. Kapha makes an excellent accountant. And with those business skills and his caring nature, Kapha makes a wonderful doctor, too.

It's good for Kapha to have a Vata woman in his corner. He could get complacent with his work, but Vata encourages him. Maybe it's her spending that motivates him, since he is more likely to be the breadwinner for the family.

Business

The home construction business would meld the talents of these two beautifully! He is a natural builder and will keep within the budget on any project. She loves to decorate and comes up with amazing design ideas.

GREAT DATES

When they said "the way to a man's heart is through his stomach," they must have been talking about a Kapha man. If Ms. Vata wants to snag a Kapha guy, all she has to do is cook a wonderful meal. It's not enough to just go to a good restaurant. Anyone can do that, and he knows it. If Mr. Kapha likes your cooking and feels like he can count on some fabulous dinners at home, he'll be yours forever!

Dates at home are great for this couple. Ms. Vata can show off her creative talents, and Mr. Kapha can get comfortable knowing he's not spending much money. This guy could probably spend every date at home, but his Vata butterfly will have him up and out and doing things that he will be thanking her for later.

Ms. Vata is impulsive and makes decisions quickly. If this is the man she wants, she goes after him ravenously. Mr. Kapha may not even know what hit him! He takes his time with such things, and it will be a challenge for this lady to get him to commit to her.

Mr. Kapha is a romantic, and of the two, will be the one who remembers the anniversary of their first date, first kiss, and first overnighter.

SENSUAL PLEASURES

The smell of cinnamon rolls baking in the oven is the biggest turn-on for the Kapha man. The fragrance of something sweet to eat just goes right through the olfactory nerve to a certain point in the brain that gets him going like nothing else! Ms. Vata can elevate her Kapha man's senses by wearing yummy-smelling perfume, like vanilla, or spice—anything warm and delicious.

When the Kapha man wants to seduce his Vata lady, he can start by wrapping her up in his arms. She loves his bear hugs and she feels safe and protected when he's taking care of her. When she relaxes like this, she is putty in his hands. They both love scented candles in the bedroom. The candles give off a romantic glow that warms a cool Vata, and the fragrance heats Kapha up more than the flame.

At Home

The Vata–Kapha house is likely to be pretty messy and disorganized. Ms. Vata is simply too busy with other things, and Mr. Kapha is so laid-back that he either doesn't notice or doesn't care. It certainly doesn't bother him enough to waste his time or energy actually cleaning up. This frustrates the sensitive Vata girl, because she notices, but just can't do much about it. The clutter adds to her anxiety and confusion and she ends up lashing out at what she perceives as a lack of support. Ah! See the conflict? Mr. Kapha thinks he is being very supportive by not expecting her to clean up herself. But what Vata really wants and needs is someone who will help balance out her weaknesses by pitching in with the organization skills she lacks. He wants to rescue her, but he can't and feels inadequate. She feels let down. . . and so it goes.

If these two can let go of their expectations and focus on the traits that they love about each other, life can be blissful. This is true for all relationships, but particularly so when opposites like Vata and Kapha get together.

Circle of Friends

Mr. Kapha has lots of friends. He has friends from "back in the day" when he was playing kick-the-can in his old neighborhood and friends he has accumulated along the way, from his high school football team to the college fraternity. Ms. Vata is amazed during the holiday season, when their mailbox bulges with greetings from all of his buddies. She can't keep track of them all! But she admires his loyalty and graciously entertains each and every one of these pals when they pass through town.

All these friends end up becoming friends with the Vata girl, which is very nice for her since her holiday card list is much shorter than her Kapha guy's. She makes friends easily, but they come and go. She loses addresses and phone numbers so it's hard for her to stay in touch. As a couple, they tend to hang out with his friends and their wives or significant others. And she gets along pretty well with anybody, so she rarely complains.

FAMILY DYNAMICS

These two make very interesting parents. The Kapha man makes a good father; he is very caring and involved in his children's activities. The Vata woman is creative in her role as mother and comes up with wonderful, fun things to do as a family. Their kids can always count on dad for a lap to sit on, and mom to keep them busy!

Their children will be either Vatas or Kaphas—so the Kapha dad has to learn to be patient with the Vata child who is always waking him up early and bouncing off the walls. The Vata mom is challenged to get her Kapha child up and moving when all he wants to do is sleep in or play video games.

If there is a Vata child and a Kapha child in the house, most likely the Kapha child will go hang out and take it easy with the Kapha dad while the two Vatas run around having fun and getting things done. Then the Vatas will come home tired and the whole family can finally relax together!

6

PITTA WOMAN & VATA MAN

Your face is illuminating the
doorway to my heart.
Tell me who you are.
—RUMI

ATTRACTION

THE PITTA WOMAN gives off a lot of heat, and because the Vata man is drawn to warmth, he's drawn to her. And why not? With her fair skin and penetrating eyes, she could be the girl of his dreams. The Vata man falls in love quickly, and he falls for the Pitta woman hard.

She sees the Vata man as tall and mysterious. He's smart, high-energy, and unpredictable. And the way he looks at her makes her blush.

When these two get together, it's hot, hot, hot! Maybe they'll meet at a club and share a sensual dance. Or maybe they'll meet at work, where the sexual tension will build until the inevitable rendezvous in the copy room. However it happens, there will be a fireworks display!

The Vata man likes to be kept guessing, and the Pitta woman does that for him. She's smart and he can talk to her. He respects her opinions and asks for them often. She likes to listen to his funny stories; she is entertained by him and has a chance to let her hair down when she is with him.

Bliss

The Pitta–Vata couple is extremely dynamic. Each is empowered by the other's complementary traits.

LIFESTYLE

The Vata man is always busy, always going, always doing—but not always with a clear sense of direction. The Pitta woman, on the other hand, knows exactly where she is going, how she will get there, and when. She plans things out and gets things done. So, if Ms. Pitta can help harness Mr. Vata's energy, he can go very far. She's good at being the leader, and he does well to follow her lead.

The Pitta woman is the kind of person who joins a club and is elected president at her second meeting. She's ambitious and likes being in charge. Her schedule is full and she keeps it that way. She's not afraid to share her opinion; her beliefs are strong, even if they are unpopular. But when she gets too focused on the details, Vata can help her to lighten up by reminding her of the "big picture."

Her Vata companion may join a club and have a great time with the people, then lose interest and join another. He has many friends, who change depending on what he's doing at the time. He's more of a spontaneous kind of guy. So when Ms. Pitta invites him to one of her social events, he'll pick up and go, even at the last minute.

Sometimes the Vata male is nervous about meeting new people or being in a new environment, but he quells his anxiety by moving around. He can seem quite fidgety at times, but it's really a coping skill that he's learned. In these situations, it's best to allow him some space. He'll be more comfortable walking around at a cocktail party than wedged in at a table between two people he doesn't know.

Exercise helps the Pitta woman keep her emotions in check. And exercise is great for helping the Vata man feel more mentally relaxed. So, it's great when they can exercise together. She tends to get competitive, which is not good for his male ego, because she'll usually win. It's better to stick to things like jogging, tai chi, or swimming-activities that these two can do together and have fun with.

Challenges

He's disorganized, she's fussy—and she sees this as a big deal. It can be a challenge for Mr. Vata to live up to Ms. Pitta's expectations of order around the house.

COMMUNICATION

A typical exchange between a Pitta woman and her Vata man might go something like this:

VM: On the way to the game next week, I'd like to stop by . . .

PW: Whoa, whoa . . . what game?

VM: You know, the Dodgers, cap night . . . I told you about it . . . anyway . . .

PW: No, I would remember something like that. When is it? It's not in my book.

VM: Thursday, I think, or Friday, anyway . . .

PW: Well, it makes a big difference—Thursday or Friday, which is it?

VM: I don't know, I have to call Paul; he has the tickets. Anyway, I want to stop by . . .

PW: Well, you have to let me know so I can write it down. Or I can look it up in the paper. Does "cap night" mean we have to wear our caps? Or what?

VM: No, it's when we get caps there, for free—it's so cool! Last
year I got two of them because . . .

PW: Yes, yes, I remember, Paul's cousin threw up, blah, blah,
blah . . . So, go on, you said you wanted to stop by
where?

VM: When?

PW: On the way to the game, you wanted to stop by where?

VM: Yeah, right . . . hmmm . . . I don't remember now. We'll
just leave a little early and I'll think of it on the way.

PW: I'm writing that down.

VM: Thanks, honey!

The Vata man thinks fast, so he's always mentally two steps ahead
of his Pitta lady. But she wants to be clear in her understanding, so
she asks for clarification, which slows him down. With practice,
these two can learn "the dance" and communicate effectively and
efficiently with each other.

EMOTIONS

The Pitta woman is sharp, intelligent, and articulate. She knows
how to choose her words carefully to do the most good, or the
most damage. Words can hurt, and she knows how to use them as
a weapon. The Vata man also uses words very well. But typically,
when his words hurt someone, it is because he spoke before
thinking about it.

Arguments between this pair are often a heated war of words,
and emotions can run high. The Pitta woman is quick to anger and
can be quite judgmental. It's easy to tell when she is angry; her
cheeks grow red and you can almost see the steam coming from
her ears. The Vata man has a low tolerance for people who don't
"get it." He has mood swings and can go from happy to harried
and back again in a single conversation.

On the plus side, Mr. Vata can be very accommodating, and Ms.
Pitta can be very adaptable. These two want to get along and there
is usually no need for confrontation. He knows how to cool her

off by responding to her needs. She knows how to calm his fears with loving reassurances.

A Word of Advice

The keyword in this relationship is *patience*. Patience, patience, patience!

SEX

If there is an argument, the make-up sex for this couple can be great. They've just got to stop talking long enough to get started. When Ms. Pitta is out of sorts, a moonlight stroll with her lover is like medicine for her.

The Vata man likes to romance his lady and he loves to be romanced himself. This is one surefire way for the Pitta woman to get his attention. Mr. Vata has an active fantasy life, and if Ms. Pitta can find her way into his imagination, it won't be long before she is in his bed.

The Pitta woman likes sex and considers herself to be very good at it. Because her Vata lover has a variable interest, she is often the aggressor, and that's usually all he needs to get in the mood. He can be very intense, which fuels her fire even more.

FOOD

This is a soup-and-salad type of a couple: he's soup and she's salad. They could probably share the same meal if she eats all the foods on the plate that are cool and heavy and he eats all the ones that are warm and light.

The Pitta woman has a strong appetite and good digestion. She can get by with the standard three meals a day, preferably with the largest meal at lunchtime, when Pitta is at its peak and the digestive fire is burning brightest.

The Vata man, however, needs to snack between meals. He has a limited supply of stored energy and needs to replenish it throughout the day. He should avoid dry foods like crackers and chips, which are harder on his system, and favor comfort foods like oatmeal and herb tea with milk.

Mung bean dahl with rice, avocados, and soy shakes with mango are all good foods that balance both Vata and Pitta and would make a good meal for this couple.

TRAVEL

The Vata man is not too crazy about traveling in general. Too much travel makes his nerves stand on end and he just can't have a good time. He has a hard time adjusting to a new time zone, climate, or unfamiliar foods, and prefers to stay near the comforts of home.

The Pitta woman loves to travel and probably travels quite a bit for her job. She can totally trust leaving her Vata guy behind to keep the home fires burning, but she'll often drag him along anyway. If he can handle the journey and not get completely worn out, the rest of the trip should be just fine.

A good compromise for this couple is to pick a spot that they both enjoy, not too far from home, where they can go when they need to get away. A vacation house is ideal, because they can keep all of their favorite foods on hand and Mr. Vata will be comfortable in familiar surroundings. His body will make the necessary adjustments more easily, and Ms. Pitta can relax more, knowing that he is in good health and able to focus on his lady.

Getaway

Go dancing! Or take dancing classes together—the class will help synchronize your moves and moods.

WORK

Many people call the Pitta woman a perfectionist, and she probably is. She knows what she wants and she knows how to get it. She is strong-willed, ambitious, and competitive. She is also very courageous and is willing to take chances in her career for her own advancement. If the Pitta woman has a weak point, it is that she is impatient and may do things in haste that she regrets later. And sometimes she works so hard that she burns herself out.

The Vata man has a lot of enthusiasm for a lot of different things. He's like the wind; he'll blow from project to project or from job to job, sometimes in quiet little breezes and other times with the huge gusts of a hurricane!

If the two of them are working together, it is better to put the Pitta in charge of the money. She's good at budgeting and will save enough to splurge on small luxuries. She's also big on finding the best bargains and getting the best deals. He tends to go through money and not even know where it disappeared to—it just takes off with the wind that seems to circulate everywhere he goes.

Business

The Pitta–Vata pair would be great collaborators in the area of sales, public speaking, writing, or Web design.

GREAT DATES

It's Ms. Pitta who likes to plan the dates for this couple. She knows what she wants and it's just easier for her to get it herself than to take a gamble and end up on some strange outing that he may arrange. Sure, she'll go along when he's got his heart set on touring some paleontology exhibit or watching one of his friend's performance art pieces. After all, she is keenly aware of fairness and doesn't want to monopolize their time with her interests alone. But she certainly enjoys knowing that all the arrangements are under control when she takes care of things herself.

Ms. Pitta does not do well in the sun. She burns easily and gets overheated quickly. So, if Mr. Vata wants to romance his lady by the water, it might be best to choose a spot by a shady stream or a waterfall, where she can keep cool.

Mr. Vata is quite creative when it comes to wooing his lady. He'll write funny verses or draw beautiful pictures—things she'll want to keep forever. Ms. Pitta is very visual, so she notices when her man is well-groomed. It may be a challenge for this Vata guy to get his act together and have his clothes pressed before a date, but it will serve him well if he takes care of such details.

SENSUAL PLEASURES

Ms. Pitta needs to turn on the heat to get her Vata guy going. Think exotic, erotic. Incense, Moroccan music, and heated massage oils all play into his fantasies.

Ms. Pitta is a visual person, so when her Vata man wants to seduce her, he can set the stage beautifully and give her lots to look at. Of course, this means starting with himself! Lots of flowers, particularly roses, whose fragrance is Pitta-balancing, will impress her. If she's racy enough, she may even get turned on having mirrors in the room.

AT HOME

The Pitta woman is diligent about writing things down. She keeps lists of things to do, places to go, items to buy, and so on. It drives her nuts that the Vata man isn't as organized; he tends to keep everything in his head.

It would be a good idea for this couple to have a housekeeper if at all possible. They need someone to keep the place together for them. The Pitta woman would rather spend her energy at work than hanging around the house. And the Vata man tends to leave a trail of stuff everywhere he goes. His mind can't function optimally unless there is order, and if he gets caught up in the clutter nothing will get done.

She can be pretty intense and insist that she get her way. He has ideas of his own; sometimes this pair does not see eye to eye. This couple has to learn to practice communicating effectively to have a happy home life, or arguments will ensue over the silliest of things.

CIRCLE OF FRIENDS

The Pitta woman is an excellent leader. She'll be the one called upon to organize the class reunion, and she'll do so happily, knowing that she really is the best one for the job. Her Pitta man will be a great help to her, coming up with fabulous original ideas to make the evening even more fun.

This couple has an address book filled with names and numbers of friends that they can call on at any time. Pitta is so good at keeping track that she becomes the social director for the couple and assists Vata with remembering the details he usually forgets. They are known as a fun couple and people love being around them.

FAMILY DYNAMICS

In this situation, mom is much more the disciplinarian and taskmaster. The kids can count on her to get them where they need to be, keep track of their crazy schedules, and provide necessary snacks and school supplies, no matter the occasion. She's definitely a take-charge kind of mom who is very involved with school activities, even when she's holding down a full-time job.

The Vata dad is fun to play with. He dreams up silly scenarios and takes the kids off on ridiculous adventures. He stretches them to be more creative and to think "outside the box." And they learn from his example, since that's the way he lives his life.

One thing this dad may teach his children is to keep a journal by their bed. Vata kids have some extraordinary dreams, and these may turn into creative writing assignments at some point. Vatas need to get in the habit of writing these things down, because they don't remember them for long. The Pitta kids may get impatient with dad, but he'll just crack a joke and get them to lighten up.

7

Pitta Woman & Pitta Man

My heart is on fire!
In my madness
I roam the desert
The flames of my passion
devour the wind and the sky.
—RUMI

Attraction

PITTAS ARE VERY visual people, so the first attraction with these two is physical—it's all about how they look to each other. They may notice each other from afar; he'll size up her figure while she scopes out his muscles. Once they make eye contact, that's it. From the first smoldering stare, they're hooked. There's not much need for conversation; they both know what they want. But they go through the ritual anyway, honoring obligatory social constraints.

That's their first mistake. If these two could just keep their mouths shut, they'd get along just fine. The problem is that they're both intelligent, ambitious, and opinionated. They're too much alike. And they both want to be in control.

It's hard to have two leaders in a relationship. Of course, in any partnership, there's some give and take, ebb and flow. But when you get two Pittas together, they keep score. And anytime you keep score, there's a winner and a loser, and each Pitta wants to be the one on top.

If they're both willing to do the work to maintain a loving relationship, this union can work out marvelously. But if they let their Pitta rage out of control, then it's just a matter of time before arguments ensue and their fiery passion burns itself out.

Bliss

The Pitta pair is passionate about work and passionate about sex. They know how to keep each other interested in the bedroom and the boardroom.

LIFESTYLE

Home life is interesting for the Pitta–Pitta pair. They both love to work, so they often have a home office, in addition to their regular workspace. When they're not doing career business in the office, they'll be busy doing other things. There is always something to plan or schedule: a party, a vacation, a holiday. Pittas like to take charge and get things done!

Pittas also love flowers and will usually have a wonderful garden in the backyard that they tend to on weekends. This isn't just a hobby for them; Pittas take everything they do seriously and want it to be the best. Water is very balancing for Pitta's hot nature, so it's great for them to have a swimming pool available and perhaps a fountain or two, for the sound of water.

Pittas tend to have firm, developed muscles—and they're very proud of them! Exercise is very balancing for Pittas; it makes them feel good, so they love it. It's great for Pittas to have access to a gym, or even have a small gym at home, so they can put themselves on a regular routine.

Competitive sports seem to attract Pittas, and you'll find many Pittas playing baseball or tennis. If the Pitta couple wants to participate in team sports, it is best if they stay on the same team! They are better off working with each other than setting up more competition between themselves than there already is.

The Pitta pair is very active and will have their social calendar booked out months in advance. If they keep the same circle of friends it will be easier for them to decide which events to attend. Otherwise, they'll have to juggle when they go to "his things" and when they go to "her things."

Challenges

When the Pitta pair argues, the whole neighborhood knows it. They have the kind of fights where dishes break and doors slam.

COMMUNICATION

Pittas are extremely discerning. They're very detail-oriented. Sometimes when they talk it almost seems like an argument because they pick at every little point. They have very strong beliefs and, hence, very strong opinions, which they freely let be known.

It is important for the Pitta type that he or she be right, so they often belabor a point until they're sure that they are fully understood. You can imagine the heated debate when two Pittas disagree about something. It's extremely frustrating and totally futile. Each competitive Pitta tries to one-up the other, and on it goes.

But when the Pittas are in sync, there no arguments; they communicate well and get a lot accomplished.

For one Pitta to talk with another, it's best to be coolly logical and organized in thought. When a Pitta can see the plan and understand what is in it for him or her, she or he is more apt to not argue. A Pitta will most likely "tweak" some of the suggestions, just to get credit for being so brilliant and contributing something essential to the "team" effort. Let your Pitta do so. It's just easier that way.

EMOTIONS

The term "hot under the collar" was probably first used to describe Pittas—they are very quick to anger. Don't ever keep a Pitta waiting. They can get impatient and irritable and it takes a lot for them to shake that mood. Pitta has a good memory for these kinds of things and will remember exactly what happened and when.

Because Pittas thinks very logically, they tend to be more in their heads than in their hearts. When they feel emotions, they want to analyze them, define them. They are very precise in their diagnosis of the situation. So the Pitta pair will talk to each other and try to figure out exactly what is going on and why each of them is having these feelings. They will be intellectual and scientific about it; if they can both agree, they can get past it.

Sometimes it is difficult for Pittas to get along with other people because they are so intolerant. Of course, Pittas don't see it this way. They think that they're right, and the other person is wrong, and thus the other person should correct his or her errors. The Pitta couple needs to avoid falling into this trap. They've got to be able to love and accept each other as they are and not try to change each other.

A Word of Advice

Spend couple-time where work is not discussed and touchy topics like politics are not brought up. Just take time to smell the roses!

SEX

Pittas don't really need a lot of romance; they can head straight for the bedroom. Both Pittas have a strong sexual desire and this may sustain their relationship for quite a while, but not forever. There will come a time when they realize that there is more to partnership than what goes on in the bedroom. And if they can't get along in other areas of their lives, they'll move on.

What makes Pitta lovers so passionate is that they find immense pleasure in pleasing each other. They're also ambitious enough to want to be "the best" at whatever they do, and sex is not an exception!

Rather than a surprise encounter, Pitta is turned on by anticipation. The Pittas like to plan their liasons and gear up for whatever is going to happen. They'll set the stage and then, at curtain time, they'll perform. Both Pittas tend to sweat a lot and will enjoy a cool shower afterward.

Pitta is aroused by aroma; the two most Pitta-balancing fragrances for massage or ambience are coconut and rose.

FOOD

Pittas do best on cool, uncooked foods. The Pitta couple can have lots of salads, raw vegetables, and fresh fruits and be very healthy. Pitta's digestion is very good, especially at midday when Pitta is at its peak. It is favorable for the largest meal of the day to be eaten around noontime.

Pittas should avoid foods that are too spicy or salty. They can be at risk for ulcers and should avoid anything too acidic. Alcohol and smoking are extremely Pitta-aggravating and should be avoided at all costs.

Pittas are frequently thirsty and should always have water or fruit juice handy. Cool drinks are good for the pair, especially during the summer.

Basic Rules for the Pitta Diet

Choose cool or warm, but not very hot foods.

Avoid salt, oil (particularly fried foods), and spicy foods.

Avoid sour foods like pickles, yogurt, and cheese. Use lemon or lime juice instead of vinegar on salads.

Avoid red meat.

Eat an abundance of salads and vegetables.

Avoid coffee and alcohol.

TRAVEL

The Pitta couple travels very well together, though they may argue about the schedule and other travel details. Each one wants to be in charge of the plans. But other than that, travel is a great way for these two to de-stress. And they do need to de-stress to stay in balance! Travel is a change of atmosphere, a break from the routine, and a stimulus to their intellect.

The best places for Pittas to go are where it is cool. If there is snow, that's even better! It is also important that there be lots of sporting activities and sightseeing, to keep these two busy.

Wherever they go, the Pitta couple should bring plenty of sunscreen. Their skin is fair and tends to burn. They are very heat-sensitive.

Getaway

Ice skating, skiing, bobsledding, and snowman-building are great fun for Pittas!

WORK

I'm going to go out on a limb here and say that the Pitta couple really shouldn't work together. It is best if they work at two different companies, preferably in two entirely different industries. If they can keep that one area of their lives separate, they'll be a lot better off.

Pittas are "thinkers"—they strategize their careers and they are fiercely ambitious. If they don't compete with one another, they'll get along nicely. If work interferes with their relationship, it could lead to disaster.

For the same reason, it's best if the Pittas leave their work at the office and not bring it home with them. Pittas can be consumed by work, and if all their energy is going into work instead of their partners, problems will arise.

If the Pittas insist on working together (for example, starting their own company), the terms of management should be clearly delineated. They can each be in charge *of different areas.* And all of their decisions need to be clearly documented in writing, so that there is no confusion and there are no arguments later.

Business

The Pitta couple would do well in a business like insurance or real estate— one where they are working as a team toward a common goal.

GREAT DATES

The two Pittas like doing the same things, so they shouldn't have trouble agreeing on where to go or what to do. They'd have great fun at an evening baseball game, where they could sit in the cool moonlight and root for their team. They'd have even more fun at a company picnic where they could play on the same team and hang out with their work friends.

If it's a special occasion, they might splurge on an all-out extravagant date, complete with limousine and vintage champagne. When anniversaries roll around, Pittas love both diamonds and pearls; these are Pitta-pacifying, particularly when set in silver or platinum.

This is one couple who loves the snow! They're both athletic and will enjoy a ski weekend away in the mountains. They've got to wear good goggles, to protect their sensitive eyes from the glare—and lots of sunscreen to avoid burning.

SENSUAL PLEASURES

The Pitta couple is especially passionate. They enjoy their sex life and are good about pleasing each other. The positive side of people with the same dominant dosha getting together is that they both respond to the same stimuli. So they can use coconut oil, rosewater fragrance, and mood lighting. If one of them likes something, chances are the other one will like it as well, so there's less guesswork involved for each of them.

Heat aggravates Pitta, so these two will want to keep the room cool. It's difficult for them in the hot summer, so they can sleep with the windows open or blast the air conditioner when they feel flushed. They might like to try rubbing sliced cucumbers on their skin. The white part of the watermelon rind is also cooling to rub on the skin and helps to pacify Pitta.

Cucumber milk is very balancing for Pitta. You can make it by blending one cup of milk (soy milk is a good substitute), about 1 to 2 inches of cucumber (about ⅓ cup), peeled and chopped, and ¼ teaspoon of sugar. You can add a little bit of saffron for flavor if you like.

AT HOME

The Pittas need to decorate with cool, soft colors to keep their Pitta in check. Blues and silvers are particularly good. It's nice for them to have a fountain in the garden, or even in the house, so they can hear the sound of water at any time. And it's great for them to have access to a swimming pool so they can take a dip, particularly on hot summer days, when Pitta is at its peak.

It's a good idea to keep the refrigerator stocked with fresh fruit and lots of salad-makings. Pittas hate to miss meals or have meals later than usual. It is important to keep their stomachs satisfied.

Pittas are happiest in cool climates and may choose to settle where they can experience cool to moderate temperatures year round.

CIRCLE OF FRIENDS

Like increases like; if you've got two Pittas together, chances are they'll be surrounded by lots of Pitta friends. And this makes sense given the places Pittas like to frequent. They love team sports, so they'll make friends with the other players on their team, for example.

Pittas are ambitious, and this can mean that they are socially ambitious as well. They'll want to attend the prominent social occasions, to see and be seen in all the right places. They're keenly aware of their place in society and prefer to be somewhere near the top. They may attend, or even organize, charity events. They'll read the society section of the newspaper and be delighted when their photo makes the page! Because both halves of the Pitta couple are like this, they'll enjoy helping each other climb the social ladder by playing the role of the "it" couple.

FAMILY DYNAMICS

The Pitta couple is bound to have Pitta kids, and they've got to be careful not to burn each other out. It will be a job just keeping track of everyone's hectic schedule—baseball practice, debate team, student council, water polo, etc.

The way for this family to approach things is to see themselves as one team, where everyone pitches in to help everyone else. They can take turns being the "star," but no one person can dominate or the whole group will get out of balance—they'll be irritable, angry, and argumentative, which is not good.

Chances are there will be a Pitta in-law or two on both sides, and they will be happiest when they feel that they are a part of the "team" as well. When they feel left out, you'll be faced with criticism. So make sure you stay in close communication with these relatives, to keep them content, loving, and supportive.

8

Pitta Woman & Kapha Man

We are the night ocean filled
with glints of light. We are the space
between the fish and the moon,
while we sit here together.
—RUMI

Attraction

THE KAPHA MAN can be exceptionally handsome. With his thick hair, full lips, and large eyes, he has boyish good looks that the Pitta woman can't resist. She sees him as a work-in-progress, full of potential.

The Kapha man sees the Pitta woman as very sensuous. Her curves and lustrous skin reveal a femininity that he finds extremely attractive. She's impressive, and he likes to be impressed. He feels that the woman he's with is a reflection of his stature and that the Pitta woman is one he can be proud to show off.

It takes some time for the Kapha man to warm up; he's not one to jump right into a new relationship. He has to think about it and test the waters for quite some time before he makes up his mind that this is the right woman for him. But once he does commit, he's in for the long haul. Sometimes this can be a problem, because if the Pitta woman decides she wants to part ways, the Kapha man will hold on with everything he has. He gets really attached and doesn't want to let go.

The Pitta woman is so project-oriented that she thinks she can fix whatever it is that doesn't appeal to her about her new Kapha mate. Usually, the problem is that she thinks she can get him to lose a little weight, or be a little more sociable and outgoing. What she'll find is that he's happy the way he is and that he doesn't want to change, not even for her.

Bliss

The Pitta–Kapha couple works well because they share a mutual respect and admiration.

LIFESTYLE

The Pitta woman is very much the social director in this relationship. She makes all the plans, and for the most part, he goes along. He'd much rather stay home, but he wants to please her, so he goes through the motions anyway. The Pitta woman finds that it can be quite a struggle after a while to get her guy going. He doesn't like the hustle-and-bustle party atmosphere that she likes, and after a few of these events, it really starts to show.

The Kapha man is very dependable and very predictable, and this may be just what the Pitta woman likes so much about him. His behavior may frustrate her at times, and she'll get angry and see him as lazy, but she respects that she can count on him. He is devoted to her and will not stray.

It really falls to the Pitta woman to motivate her Kapha man. He needs outside stimulation to do just about anything. If left to his own devices, he'll take the easiest road and coast the whole way. But Pitta can light a fire under him, and with her ambition and support he can accomplish more than he ever would on his own.

He needs her encouragement in every area of his life. She can help him to eat right, exercise, and to go for that promotion and salary hike.

Of course, he has the ability to accomplish all this or it wouldn't happen, and the Pitta woman knows this. It's just her job to bring out the best in him, and she does.

The Kapha man's role is to help his Pitta lady mellow out a little bit. If it weren't for him, she would probably never sit still. But instead of working 24/7, she's now content to sit cozily on the couch with her Kapha honey in the evenings. He is actually good for her health. She's the Type A personality and he's Type B. She can definitely learn some tips on cooling down from this laid-back guy.

Challenges

The Pitta woman can be critical, and the Kapha man is sensitive and tends to take things personally. She needs to learn to be a little softer around him, and he needs to develop a thicker skin around her.

COMMUNICATION

The Kapha man tends to take the long way around when telling a story or making a point. His speech is slow and often monotonous, most likely because he is thinking it through even as he speaks.

The Pitta woman, on the other hand, is very clear and precise in her choice of words. She's direct and authoritative. She is articulate and easy to understand; she doesn't cloud the issue at hand with unnecessary embellishments.

When the Pitta woman is paired with the Kapha man, she must be patient. This is often a struggle for her, but one she must endure to maintain harmony in the relationship. If she can learn to nod lovingly as her Kapha mate goes on and on about something she sees as irrelevant, he will feel heard and respected.

What the Kapha man needs to learn in this relationship is not to take things personally. Ms. Pitta will snap and stomp, but it doesn't necessarily have anything to do with what Mr. Kapha said or did. She just automatically reacts, and sometimes her anger gets the best of her. The Kapha man can be very sensitive, but he needs to get over it if he is going to get along with this fiery lady.

The Kapha man doesn't like conflict and avoids it at any cost. He'd just rather not argue or stir up trouble. He'll listen to others' opinions—but don't think you are going to change his. Once he's made up his mind about something, that's it. There's no moving this one. He is as stubborn as they come.

EMOTIONS

The Pitta woman can have quite a temper, and if she holds her feelings in, it can result in health problems such as ulcers and migraine headaches. If she lets out bottled-up feelings, it can be explosive. So it's best to just let her vent as things come up. Hopefully, with Kapha's influence, she will learn over time to express herself tactfully and unemotionally.

Ms. Pitta is a fireball who freely shares her ideas and opinions. She likes stirring the pot, getting people involved, and talking about important issues. She can be aggressive, but only because she is so strong in her beliefs.

The Kapha man manages to stay calm in any situation, no matter how disastrous. He's the rock that everyone leans on. In an emergency, this is the guy you want by your side. He's solid and strong. His large shoulders are good for crying on.

Mr. Kapha can be very sentimental. He has good long-term memory and will remember the smallest details of your first meeting. This seems sweet when Kapha is in balance, but when he's out of balance, he can appear possessive.

When things don't go his way, the Kapha man is easily depressed. It's best for his Pitta partner to bring this to his attention before he sinks into a black abyss. Getting him up and moving and involved will go a long way toward helping him overcome his dark mood.

A Word of Advice

It is important for this couple to clearly define their roles and expectations in the relationship, particularly when it comes to household chores and expenses.

SEX

The Pitta woman and Kapha man are very sexually compatible. He may be slow to arouse, but once he gets going, he's got a lot of stamina. His passion lasts a long time. The Pitta woman likes this. She considers herself to be somewhat of a sexual connoisseur and she appreciates his endurance. She may need to teach him a few things in the finesse department, but he is an eager student.

The Kapha man is very affectionate and loves to cuddle. He feels very lucky and happy that a beautiful Pitta babe is in his arms and he doesn't want to let her go. She might try to wiggle away, but it's only because she gets too hot. If he wants to hold her close, it's best to keep the room temperature cool enough for her liking.

Ms. Pitta has a strong sex drive and she can depend on Mr. Kapha to cooperate. She may be the initiator more often than not, but they are both willing and capable participants.

FOOD

Food is sometimes a contentious issue between these two, mostly because the Pitta woman has to tell the Kapha man what he can and cannot eat. When it comes to his diet, Mr. Kapha has no willpower. Food is important to him, and he indulges in the foods he loves. Unfortunately, they are the foods that he really shouldn't have. She knows this, and he fights it.

He is jealous that his beautiful Pitta partner is satisfied with a

salad. He can't do that. Not only does he want the meat and potatoes, he wants the butter and the gravy to go with them. And in his
book, no meal is complete without dessert! This behavior frustrates
Ms. Pitta, who watches his waistline expand. She prides herself on
her appearance and wishes that he paid more attention to his.

So the two must reach some sort of a compromise to keep each
other happy. They can work on finding lower-fat foods and recipes
that they will both enjoy. And she can help him to avoid overeating
by portioning out his meals. Everything in moderation!

Spicy dishes are good for Kapha, because they are stimulating
and help him feel satisfied. They're not so good for Pitta, who over-
heats easily. He needs warm food and drinks; it's better for her to
have cooler food and drinks. Chances are that at a restaurant, they'll
order completely different dishes.

TRAVEL

If you ask him, Mr. Kapha will say that he doesn't necessarily
like to travel, but that he always has a good time when he goes.
Travel is wonderful for Kapha! This is a great way for this couple
to spend time together. Ms. Pitta likes to be on the go and she'll
plan an exciting trip. Mr. Kapha can just sit back and enjoy because
she's taken care of all the details.

He prefers to be in warm climates, but he'll be okay as long as
he dresses appropriately. Ms. Pitta prefers a cooler climate, but if
there is any sunshine, she'll need her sunglasses because she is very
sensitive to the light. She'll also want to bring sunscreen to protect
her fair skin.

The Pitta woman needs to be careful not to overschedule her
Kapha man. He needs downtime. He also needs plenty of time to
sleep. He's like a hibernating bear; his sleeps are long and deep. And
if he doesn't get enough, he's grumpy.

He's not a big spender, but being the romantic that he is, the
Kapha man will make sure his lady gets a nice little souvenir to
remember their trip together.

Getaway

These two will have a wonderful time on a cruise ship headed just about anywhere! There are plenty of social activities to keep her happy, and the pace is relaxed enough to keep him content.

WORK

The Kapha man tends to have fairly simple tastes, but the Pitta woman is ambitious enough for both of them! Because of her, he'll find that he earns more money and gets further ahead in his career than he ever would alone. The Pitta woman is competitive, and she'll want to make as much money as her Kapha mate, or more! So she'll work harder and they'll both be sitting pretty.

The difference between the two is that the Kapha man likes to take lots of breaks. He needs vacation time and loves to relax. The Pitta woman, on the other hand, could be a workaholic if she weren't monitored. But Kapha will take care of that and make sure that she's home with him. He'll remind her to put their relationship first, and he'll do this by example.

Business

If the Pitta woman runs for political office, the Kapha man is her ideal partner. No one could be more supportive or encouraging.

GREAT DATES

Ms. Pitta may be a bit taken aback when Mr. Kapha pulls out his "two for one" coupon on one of their dinner dates. But when she realizes that he doesn't expect her to split the check with him, as so many other men have, she'll be more forgiving. And when they start talking business and finances and she learns how well his investments are doing, she'll start to admire his frugality.

Other than that, he's a true romantic. He'll choose a nice place and treat her like a lady. Sometimes Pitta will wonder what all the fuss is about. She tries to figure him out. But there's nothing to figure out—that's just the way he is.

If the Pitta lady wants to woo the Kapha man, she can present herself as a good investment, too. He'll like that she's smart and ambitious, and that she can take care of herself. But he'll want her to take some time to take care of him, so she can't place her work above their relationship.

The element of water is something that Pitta and Kapha have in common; a date out sailing or whale-watching would be ideal. They need to pack a picnic, so Pitta doesn't miss a meal and Kapha can snack when the hunger pangs hit.

SENSUAL PLEASURES

Ms. Pitta can lure her Kapha man with seductive scents—he's particularly susceptible to cinnamon, basil, and musk. She can have this simmering in an aroma pot, or brush a few drops of essential oil through her hair.

Mr. Kapha can bring flowers to make a favorable impression on his Pitta lady. He'll probably cut them from his own garden to save money, but that's fine with her. She'll love the sweet gesture.

The Kapha man is very loving and he'll get lots of warmth from his Pitta mate.

AT HOME

Decor can be difficult for this couple because color-wise, they're on opposite ends of the spectrum. She needs things cool and calming; he needs things warm and stimulating. The way around this is to use a clean, neutral palette, punctuated with accents that suit each of them.

Ms. Pitta can also keep her personal space, a home office for example, filled with the cooling colors that she craves, while her Kapha man can warm up his space with rich woods and bright, bold colors. Since they both love the water, they will enjoy beautiful watercolor paintings, particularly seascapes, hanging on their walls. It'd be great if they could have a little vacation retreat on a lake somewhere, which would motivate Kapha to travel and give Pitta a place to go to, to get away from work.

CIRCLE OF FRIENDS

The Kapha man is mellow; he gets along fine with all of Pitta's work friends. They think she's lucky to have a man who dotes on her so much. Mr. Kapha prefers to entertain at home, but Ms. Pitta would rather go out and make new contacts and connections. The Pitta woman can be a perfectionist, so when this couple does have friends over, she spends hours getting everything ready; it is important to her that everything be "just right." If she gives her Kapha man specific jobs to do to help out, he will methodically get them done—she just shouldn't be in a hurry, because he always takes his time.

Pitta is aggravated by a lot of things that you usually find at parties: alcohol, spicy or salty foods, and excessive activity. So, this couple really needs to keep things more on the mellow side so that Ms. Pitta doesn't get too stressed out from her role as hostess. And they need to be sure that Mr. Kapha doesn't overdo it by overeating or indulging in too many heavy foods, or his Kapha will get out of whack and he'll be grumpy.

FAMILY DYNAMICS

The Kapha dad is a pretty laid-back, easy-to-get-along-with kind of guy. He's happy to play Papa Bear and loves wrestling with his little cubs. These cubs need to watch out when their old man is sleeping, though, because if they wake him up before he's ready, he'll growl.

The Pitta mom sets the rules of the house, and the kids know to comply. Her Pitta kids will want to go to work with her, or ask what jobs they can do to earn money all the time. The Kapha kids will take their birthday checks and sock them away, so they'll always have money in the bank. The Pitta kids are competitive, so there may be some sibling rivalry. But that rarely occurs with Kapha kids, who are affectionate and loving and just happy to hang out with the family.

9

Kapha Woman & Vata Man

Birdsong, wind
the water's face.
Each flower, remembering the smell:
I know you're close by.
—RUMI

Attraction

THE KAPHA WOMAN is soft and feminine. She has thick, wavy hair and gorgeous big eyes with thick lashes. Elizabeth Taylor, arguably the most beautiful woman in the world, is Kapha-dominant.

The Kapha woman is generally shy, so it is up to the more out-going Vata man to approach her. The Vata man is attracted to this gentle beauty as a butterfly is drawn to a flower. She doesn't have to do much to get his attention—just be available. Like a flower, she is rooted to the earth. Like a butterfly, he flies with the wind.

Mr. Vata is unpredictable and this amuses fair Kapha. She is stable and blooms where she is planted. The Vata man finds this warm and inviting, but is it enough to keep his attention for the long haul? He can be flighty, and sweet Kapha deserves someone who will stick around. Then again, she is very forgiving and will put up with a lot from her man.

Bliss

The home of the Kapha–Vata pair is warm and homey, and at the same time has all the latest and greatest technological perks.

LIFESTYLE

The Vata man is in constant motion. He's fidgety and it's hard for him to sit still. This is in direct contrast to the Kapha woman, who is calm and serene.

He likes to go out and do things; she is more of a homebody. He gets bored easily and needs lots of new and different experiences to keep him interested. She is content to cuddle up and read a book while a loaf of bread bakes in her oven.

What these two really need is some sort of a balance. Because Kapha craves routine, they could make a schedule that accommodates both their needs. For instance, on Monday, Wednesday, and Friday they stay in; and on Tuesday, Thursday, and Saturday they go out. On nights they go out, the activities will have to be spontaneous, as Vata is not good at planning ahead. So there will definitely be some surprises, which will keep him on his toes.

Although Vata seems to be a bottle of nervous energy, his reserves do not run deep. He doesn't just get tired—he gets exhausted. Kapha can help him to rest and fuel up in between all of his countless excursions.

And although Kapha could sit happily Buddha-like all day, she has an enormous energy reserve that needs to go somewhere. If she doesn't get up and go, she is likely to gain weight. Vata can help with this by stimulating her interest and coming up with fun things for them to do together.

Challenges

These two need to be careful to not assume the roles of parent and child with each other. The Kapha woman can be very mothering, and the Vata man can be childlike.

COMMUNICATION

This pair has a unique style of communication: He talks and she listens! Mr. Vata is never at a loss for words. He has a lot to say and he usually manages to say it all. Ms. Kapha listens lovingly, taking it all in. By the time she can get a word in edgewise, she's had a lot of time to mull over the information and can make thoughtful and insightful comments.

When the Kapha woman speaks, the Vata man tends to interrupt. He's not doing this to be rude; it's just that his brain is running ahead of her tongue and he can't help but blurt it all out. He also tends to yawn a lot, but she should not take this personally either. Vata is made up of air, and this helps him to get oxygen to his super-busy brain. This is one reason why Vatas tend to have dry mouths and need lots of water.

Although the Vata man talks a lot, most of his speech is superficial. He has a lot of ideas and dreams, but he can't possibly follow through on all of them. He has lots of projects that he started with good intentions but will never finish. When Kapha accepts that this is just the way he is, she'll get used to doing things like calling the plumber to reconnect the pipes that Mr. Vata has taken apart.

The Kapha woman, in contrast to her mate, is very diligent and sincere. She means what she says and is true to her word. She is very reliable. The Vata man knows that he can always count on her, and that means a lot to him.

EMOTIONS

It takes a long time for the Kapha woman to give her heart, but when she does, it's forever. She's a true romantic and totally devoted to her man. She is very reasonable and doesn't have unrealistic expectations of her Vata man, so she is never disappointed with him.

The Vata man may commit to forever and then change his mind. His moods change often; he goes with the wind. He likes to think of himself as open-minded and flexible. Some would say that he is flaky and inconsiderate. The Kapha woman, steady and stable, can be a good influence on her Vata man. She can teach him to empathize and open his eyes to the consequences of his actions. He is usually anxious about bringing out his more vulnerable side, but she makes him feel safe.

A Word of Advice

In any relationship, there must be an element of compromise, and in the Kapha–Vata relationship, compromise is even more important. These two can be opposites, yet they can also lend the balance that each of them needs in their lives.

SEX

The Kapha woman is a major challenge for the Vata man. She doesn't jump into bed with just any guy. She doesn't fall victim to lust. She takes her time and gets to know a person and thinks through her decisions carefully.

The Vata man is turned on by the thrill of the chase. The process of love is exciting for him. He loves to woo the beautiful Kapha and spares no expense to garner her affections. He's got his creativity going for him, so she can expect a lot more than the typical flowers and candy. He'll find the exotic locales, the most unusual aphrodisiacs, and dance just for her.

His attention delights Ms. Kapha and her smile is his reward. It is hard for her to resist a man who will do backflips just to get her to look his way. When she finally gives in to her Vata man's charms, she embraces him just as he is, antics and all.

The Vata man soon discovers that his efforts were well worth it. She is more caring and attentive to him than he ever imagined she could be.

FOOD

Left to their own bad habits, this couple would end up looking like the pair in the nursery rhyme "Jack Sprat." She gains weight easily and it's hard for her to take it off. He loses weight easily and it's harder for him to put it on. But if they stick to their Ayurvedic diets, they can remain in balance and be healthy and happy.

Both the Kapha and Vata need warm, cooked foods. She needs to avoid sweets, so he shouldn't tempt her with those creamy truffles that she loves. They can both eat spicy foods and can find plenty of things at Thai and Indian restaurants that are good for them.

It is fine for Vata to graze between meals, and he probably needs to snack in order to keep up his energy. But Kapha should just stick to the three-meals-a-day rule. She has plenty of reserved energy, so she shouldn't feel hungry enough to snack. If she caves in, it's only because she wants to eat, not because she needs to eat.

TRAVEL

Both the Kapha woman and the Vata man prefer warmer climates, which makes it easier for them when choosing a vacation destination. Kapha can pretty much go anywhere, as long as it's not too humid. Vata just needs to avoid cold and dry. The desert is not a good choice for him, but she'd probably love it.

Although the Kapha woman has no trouble with planes, trains, or boats, the Vata man can get physically ill from most modes of transportation. It's the movement, which aggravates Vata and throws him out of balance. The slower the vehicle, the less likely he is to get sick. So it's best if they can find somewhere closer to home, maybe within driving distance, to go for their vacations.

If he does get sick, Ms. Kapha will take good care of her man. She's a natural nurturer and knows just what to do to make him feel better. Usually some rest, to help him adapt to the new surroundings, and some water, are all he needs.

Getaway

An afternoon exploring different museums is a great way for these two to spend time together.

WORK

Just as the Kapha woman is loyal to her partner, she is loyal to her job. She is likely to stay with the same company, and certainly the same career, for a long, long time. Kaphas do well in the medical field or in education, where they can put their people skills to good use.

Meanwhile, the Vata man will probably have several different jobs over a short period of time. He likes to change jobs and may even change careers once or twice. He may juggle more than one job in more than one area.

Mr. Vata hates routine and works best when he is working for himself. It is difficult for him to be confined to an office and a set schedule. It is best for him if his activities during the day are varied, and if he has a creative outlet through his work.

The Vata man seems to go through money quickly. He's a spender rather than a saver. He lives paycheck to paycheck, playing it by ear and hoping to hit the jackpot. His investment strategy is a weekly lottery ticket.

The Kapha woman, on the other hand, is more a saver than a spender. She is extremely prudent with her money and usually has a nice nest egg put away at an early age. Of the two of them, she is the one with the retirement account.

Business

A home-based business would be great for this couple. A travel agency or an Internet company is ideal.

GREAT DATES

The Kapha woman will want to have her Vata man over to her house. She'll show him how comfortable it is, and how comfortable he can be there. The Vata man will want to take his lady out on the town. He'll show her how fun and entertaining he can be, and how much he can make her laugh. And she does laugh when she's with him, which is very attractive to her.

One great date would be to go kite-flying in the park. She can pack a yummy picnic lunch for them and he can run around playing the clown trying to get the kite in the air. When he collapses onto her soft picnic blanket, he can rest his head in her lap and look into her big beautiful eyes. "What could be better?" he will think.

Ms. Kapha will feel uncomfortable when Mr. Vata spends money on extravagant gifts for her. He will score more points if he writes her a poem or a love song and shows her a growing account balance. Security is important to this lady, and she doesn't want to think that she's going to have to compensate for Vata's irresponsible spending habits.

SENSUAL PLEASURES

Vata responds to touch, so Ms. Kapha should hold his hand, stroke his cheek, and brush his hair with her hand. He loves this and loves being near her.

Kapha responds the most to taste and smell, and also needs stimulation to get the libido going. One way to do this is to block out the other senses. Her Vata man can blindfold her and have her play a guessing game while he feeds her luscious foods like chocolate-covered strawberries or peaches with cream. When this experience proves pleasurable—and it will—she will trust him, and the games can continue in the bedroom.

AT HOME

Yellows and golds are balancing for both Vata and Kapha, so these are nice colors to have in the decorating scheme for this couple. They tend to spend lots of time in the kitchen together, so Mr. Vata will like to have the latest and greatest appliances on hand to tinker with. Ms. Kapha will do most of the actual cooking, but he'll still have to have a fancy juice machine, a bread machine, and a food processor with all the accessories. He enjoys figuring out how all this stuff works. And he likes shopping for them, too.

Another "appliance" that keeps Vata home with Kapha is the computer. He can be endlessly fascinated with all kinds of software programs. Ms. Kapha might have to keep an eye on him to make sure that he doesn't get too distracted with the games and the Internet. He can be really talented at graphic design, writing music, or script-writing, and when he applies his computer savvy to one of these areas, amazing things happen. Ms. Kapha encourages him-she'd much rather have him home, even if he's mesmerized at the computer screen, than out running around.

To get Vata away from the computer and Kapha out of the kitchen, these two can establish a ritual of taking an evening walk together. The walk will help his digestion after dinner and keep her on a regular exercise schedule.

CIRCLE OF FRIENDS

Ms. Kapha has her little circle of girlfriends dating back from her days in the Girl Scouts. It's good for her to keep in contact with them and have girl-time just to relax and take a break from Vata's constant activity.

Vata makes friends, and changes friends, often. He'll be bringing them home to show off his lady's cooking and she'll graciously oblige. She loves to see him enthusiastic, and he always perks up when he gets the chance to entertain.

FAMILY DYNAMICS

The Vata kids are going to run circles around the Kapha kids. They'll do all the talking at the dinner table, so the Kapha kids will have to learn early on how to get a word in edgewise. They make good siblings, because they balance each other out. The Kapha kids get the Vatas to mellow out and relax a little, and the Vata kids get the Kaphas up and running around outside. If there's a cold going around at school, the Vatas will catch it first and bring it home to the Kaphas—but the Kaphas have a much stronger immune system, so they won't always get sick.

The Kapha woman is an excellent mother and makes the job her top priority. She is very nurturing and makes sure all of her children's needs are met. The Vata dad is one fun guy and has a great time acting like a kid himself and being goofy with his brood.

10

Kapha Woman
&
Pitta Man

My heart has burned with passion
and has searched forever
for this wondrous beauty
that I now behold.
—RUMI

Attraction

THE PITTA MAN knows what he wants and he knows how to get it. When he sets his sights on the Kapha woman, she doesn't stand a chance! But Kapha is cautious and wise. It takes time to win her over completely. If the Pitta man steadies his pace and attends to the rituals of courtship, his Kapha will fall deeply in love with him.

Ms. Kapha, with her graceful manner and calm demeanor, is a welcome contrast to Mr. Pitta's high-stress way of life. He sees her as a refuge and seeks solace in the comfort of her arms. She demands nothing of him, and with her, he can relax and be more of himself.

The fiery energy that circulates through the Pitta man is what sparks the Kapha woman's interest. She likes that he goes after what he wants, and it makes her happy that he wants her. She is extremely patient, so if the Pitta man catches her eye first, she will make her moves slowly and tentatively. She is a bit shy but extremely charming.

Bliss

This couple can achieve their goals and live in financial security. They can make smart decisions together regarding investments.

LIFESTYLE

The Kapha woman has deep roots. Chances are that she has kept some of the same friends that she had back in elementary school. She remembers all of her teachers. It's unlikely that she'll move too far away from where she grew up, and if she does, a piece of her home will always reside in her heart.

Friends and family are very important to Ms. Kapha, and she'll keep track of birthdays and special occasions. Mr. Pitta feels lucky to be so doted on and cared for. He enjoys the stability that she provides for him.

Although family is important to the Pitta man, it doesn't always come first. He is very ambitious and has lofty career goals. He is usually juggling his family, career, social life, and community responsibilities, and sometimes he drops a ball. He often feels pressured, but most of that pressure is coming from himself. He is always striving for more.

Mr. Pitta is into sports big-time! They are a great physical outlet for him. He needs to be out in the fresh air, running, playing, swimming, and socializing. He likes to play competitively—many professional athletes are Pitta-dominant types. It takes a Pitta fire to make it to that elite level in such a highly competitive field.

It's really great for the Kapha woman to get out there and exercise with her Pitta honey. She's no competition for this guy, but he loves it when she shares his interests, and he loves to see that she is taking care of herself. When Kapha lets herself get lazy, she can pack on the pounds. Exercise is an important part of keeping Kapha in shape. Mr. Pitta is proud of his appearance—he worked hard for those muscles! So he is bound to take notice of his lady's figure, too.

Challenges

Mr. Pitta can be judgmental and Ms. Kapha tends to take things personally. He becomes impatient when she sulks. He needs to keep his cool more and she needs to understand that he's not trying to be insensitive.

COMMUNICATION

It sometimes sounds as though the Pitta man is looking for an argument. He loves to talk, debate, and make his opinions known. He can be pretty pushy when it comes to his hot-button issues. He likes to show off his intellect.

All this does nothing for the mild-mannered Kapha woman, who would rather avoid conflict at all costs. She's smart and has her own opinions, which she'd prefer to keep to herself. If the Pitta man thinks he has convinced her of anything, he's got another thing coming. She'll smile sweetly and nod to keep him from pushing any further, but it's highly unlikely that she'll change her mind. She does what she wants to do and what her conscience tells her is the right thing. It's best for Mr. Pitta to just take this in stride and not get himself worked up needlessly.

Pitta thinks with his head and Kapha thinks with her heart. He likes to plan things in advance and to know where he's headed. He looks at the logic of things, to see if it makes sense to him. Kapha needs time to digest things. She likes to mull things over before making any big decisions. She does not like to be rushed into anything.

These different decision-making processes could be a good balance for each other, if the two approach it the right way. They need to consult each other and look at all of the likely scenarios. Pitta needs to slow down and listen more. His impatience only makes his lady want to retreat. Kapha needs to be more open-minded and expressive about her feelings.

As much as Kapha resists change, Pitta can usually talk her into it. And when she's made an informed decision, she can feel good about whatever the outcome may be.

EMOTIONS

The Kapha woman is extremely loyal and dependable. Her feelings are very slow to change. Once she falls in love, that's it—it's forever, to her. She's a private person; some might perceive this as passivity. But try to uproot her and you're in for a fight. She's firm in her convictions.

The Pitta man is aggressive. He lets his feelings show. He has a temper and this could upset Ms. Kapha, who is generally even-keeled. He gets excited easily and he reacts strongly.

When they have a fight, it's Kapha who sulks and turns inward. She gets depressed and looks for comfort in the kitchen. Pitta lashes out with his frustration and says things he'll later regret. It's hard to get Kapha out of her rut once she's in it, but Pitta has the capacity to be sensitive and compassionate, and once he's cooled down, he's better able to figure out how to make them both happy.

A Word of Advice

It would be a great idea to set up a home office so that Mr. Pitta could spend some of his time working at home and be around his family more, which would please his Kapha mate.

SEX

The Kapha woman's bedroom is likely to be flirty and feminine. She's a creature of comfort, so she likes lots of pillows on her bed and a big, fluffy comforter draped across it. She goes to all this effort, and the Pitta man needs just a mattress and a sheet!

The Pitta man likes to sleep naked. He gets too hot at night with so many layers. The Kapha woman loves the idea of lounging around in pajamas. Her favorite part of the day is when she gets to kick off her shoes, slip on her robe, and just relax!

The Kapha–Pitta pair is very compatible sexually. His passion stimulates her and she melts at his caress. He likes that she doesn't get worn out easily and that she's content to take her time and go with the flow.

As far as children go, the Kapha woman is extremely fertile and the Pitta man is very virile. They can have lots of children and should practice diligent birth control if they prefer a smaller family!

FOOD

Because both the Pitta man and Kapha woman like food a lot, they're likely to spend a great deal of their time in the kitchen. The Kapha woman will find out just what her honey likes to eat and make him some marvelous meals. He tends to go for high-protein foods such as meats, beans, and eggs. She loves carbohydrates and feasts on pasta, breads, and rice.

This couple has to take care with their diets or they'll both end up overweight. The Kapha woman should avoid sugar altogether. She can sweeten her tea with honey, as an alternative. The Pitta man can have some sugar, but it is best to get it from fruits rather than from cakes and candies. Honey is a no-no for him. It's sticky, which is one of the properties of Pitta, so it's Pitta-aggravating. They can both eat salads, but she should not have too much oil or fat in her dressings.

It's good for them to walk after their meals to stimulate digestion and help burn off some calories. It is also better for them to eat a smaller-sized meal earlier in the evening so they have plenty of time to digest and assimilate the food before they go to sleep. Lunch, at around noon, should be the largest meal of the day.

TRAVEL

Chances are most of the trips that the Pitta man takes will be work-related. So most of the time, he can leave his Kapha lady at home, which is just fine with her. But it's really good for her when she goes along! Travel is very stimulating and Kapha needs that to stay in balance.

Whenever they do go away, the Pitta man will handle all the arrangements. He loves to plan and see where he can get the best deals. He's very detail-oriented and knows how to handle frequent-flier coupons and the like.

They can spend their days with lots of sightseeing and touring around for him, and then their evenings at great restaurants with lots of romance and quiet for her. It'd be ideal for them to stay at a hotel with a spa where they can get massages, which are great for both of them.

Getaway

Glide in a gondola and kiss under the bridges along the way, or row on a serene lake and snack on grapes and strawberries.

WORK

The Kapha woman loves children and loves to work with children. She's a kind, patient teacher and a wonderful mother. When she is the head of the household, she is a very good provider. She knows how to balance budgets and stretch a dollar.

Although the Pitta man is ambitious and hardworking, he should turn over his paycheck directly to his Kapha mate, because she is better at handling the money. She is very good at saving and will make sure that the two of them retire rich! She likes security and is very prudent.

He's a moderate spender but tends to splurge on luxuries. He might drive up in a red Corvette one day, which most people will chalk up to a midlife crisis purchase. But in reality, it's his Pitta all fired up. He always wants the best, so sometimes he'll spend more on things than he really should.

If they end up having a lot of kids, they're going to need a lot of money! But with him working and her saving, that shouldn't be a problem. This tends to be a traditional household. She loves to spend time with children and he loves to work. He can deal with business at the office with great aplomb, but he doesn't have as much patience when it comes to the children.

Business

If Mr. Pitta has political aspirations, the Kapha woman can help get him there. These two would excel at anything having to do with health care or education: a tutoring center, or a doctor's or veterinarian's office, for example.

GREAT DATES

Mr. Pitta likes to take special care in arranging all the details for a great date with his lady. He's punctual, which she appreciates, though she may keep him waiting while she finishes getting ready. He's not Mr. Romance, but he works hard at reaching his goals, and if Ms. Kapha is his goal, he needs to be at the top of his game.

Ms. Kapha loves gardening and flowers, so it would be a great idea to take her to a botanical garden. Mr. Kapha is balanced by the fragrance of rose, so the two will likely spend a lot of time in the rose garden. This is nice because they can walk and talk and get to know each other in a beautiful natural setting.

Afterward they can spend time at a little bistro, with good food and candlelight—maybe some Italian place where she can have pasta and he can have an antipasto salad. Then they can drive off in his convertible and park somewhere under the stars.

SENSUAL PLEASURES

This is the perfect couple for a "bed of roses." It's best if it is a surprise, but it doesn't matter which half of the couple initiates it. Rose petals are the ultimate aphrodisiac. Collect them from fully-bloomed flowers; the more, the better! (Four dozen works well for a queen-sized bed.) Then turn down the bed and spread them all over the mattress evenly. Take note that red roses tend to stain, so either use sheets that you don't mind staining, or use lighter-colored petals. Pinks and yellows are really pretty together and create a soft, romantic glow. The combination of the silky petals and their intoxicating fragrance is enough to keep any Kapha woman and Pitta man mesmerized all night long—and not just with the flowers, either!

Because water is so cooling and balancing for Pitta, Ms. Kapha might try a version of this in the bathtub for her Pitta man when he's feeling out of sorts. Just run a cool bath, and let the petals float on top. Turn down the lights and keep a fluffy towel nearby. He'll emerge content as a kitten.

AT HOME

This couple will spend a lot of time in the backyard. He'll want to set up a basketball court for himself and the kids, and she'll want space for a vegetable and herb garden. They need to make sure there are plenty of shaded areas, so the Pittas can avoid the sun. It would be nice to have a pool or a fountain to keep the place feeling cool in the summer. The Kapha kids will want to have friends over a lot, and this will probably be the house where they all congregate. It's a good idea to keep some turkey-dogs on hand for the occasional impromptu barbeque!

If these two argue, it's usually because she's so sentimental and he's so . . . not! She's emotional and he's intellectual. Each should look at what the partner has got, rather than what he or she lacks. He may not be romantic, but he is passionate. She may seem a little clingy, but she is fiercely loyal.

CIRCLE OF FRIENDS

Once they've settled down, Ms. Kapha will make friends with all of the other mothers at the kids' schools. The kids' friends' parents will then become the couple's friends and they'll do a lot of socializing this way. Mr. Pitta likes this because it's a good opportunity for him to make business contacts, particularly if he is in any type of sales position. Ms. Kapha likes having friends over, especially when the kids are involved, because she likes to keep her family close to home.

FAMILY DYNAMICS

Mom is patient, Dad is strict. The Pitta kids are competitive, the Kapha kids are more laid-back. A lot of family time will be spent driving to the various games that each of the kids and their teams are involved with. The Pitta dad will likely coach some of the teams and have great fun with the job, especially when one of his athletic Pitta kids is on his team. The Kapha kids may get involved with sports, but they're doing it more for the social atmosphere than for the game itself. They just like being on the team and don't mind sitting on the bench. Kapha Mom never misses a game and comes with a cooler stocked with drinks and snacks "just in case!"

11

Kapha Woman
&
Kapha Man

Between my love and my heart
things were happening which
slowly, slowly
made me recall everything.
—RUMI

Attraction

THERE'S A WELL-KNOWN fable in which a tortoise and a hare had a race. The hare, though favored to win, became overconfident because he underestimated the tenacity of his opponent. The tortoise was victorious, because, as the moral goes, "slow and steady wins the race."

I'm sure that the tortoise enjoyed the hare's company, but when he went home that night, he was probably really glad to have another tortoise who appreciated all of his strong points, someone he didn't have to prove himself to.

Kaphas are very much like the tortoise when it comes to relationships. They tend to be attracted to one another because they love to feel understood. They are very sweet people, kind and sensitive. They are also grounded in reality. They can see themselves in another Kapha and relate to one another with few words. They're completely comfortable together.

When two Kaphas get together, it's like a savory stew simmering in a Crock-Pot. It's not the fireworks that you get with Pittas or the "rush" that Vatas experience. Instead, the relationship is gentle, patient, loving, and warm. It takes a long time to get there, but then it lasts forever.

Bliss

The Kapha pair is totally devoted to one another. They are both committed for the long run, and they understand what that means.

LIFESTYLE

Because Kaphas love to spend time at home, this couple will have a really beautiful home. They invest a lot of their time and money making their home their sanctuary. They would rather be home than just about anywhere.

But too much of this can get Kapha lazy and "stuck." Kaphas need lots of stimulation to stay in balance, and they can't get that sitting on the couch watching TV. So Kaphas need to force themselves to get out and mingle, see the world!

Even though Kaphas are shy, they tend to have very close, very loyal friends. It is great for them to use their home to entertain, and Kaphas are wonderfully charming hosts, very focused on taking care of the needs of all of their guests.

Kaphas also need stimulation in the form of exercise. The best exercises for them are the ones that really get them moving, like bodybuilding, running, and biking. If this couple can use exercise as a way to spend time together, it will be very beneficial for both of them.

Kaphas are often very religious, and because they enjoy routine, they can usually be found in church every weekend. If there is a later service, that's the one they'll attend; they love to sleep late whenever possible!

Challenges

Too much routine can lead to complacency. The Kapha couple needs to "mix it up" once in a while!

COMMUNICATION

Kaphas like to think about things for a long time before coming to a final conclusion. But once they've made up their minds, it is difficult to get them to change. Kaphas are better listeners than talkers. They need time to process information before they have to give constructive feedback. It is hard for Kaphas to formulate ideas and answers off the top of their heads, and if you push them on it, they will either clam up or ramble on and on. However, when you let them mull over things for a while, you will receive some thoughtful and wise comments and/or advice.

When Kaphas talk to each other, they understand the special Kapha thought process and allow each other that extra time. Because of this, there are fewer arguments and disagreements. This tends to be a very congenial household.

Of course, Kapha is the most stubborn of the doshas, so if there is some disagreement, they'll each dig in their heels. The trick is for the two to find some common ground and build from there. Compromise is possible, and Kapha is usually reasonable and forgiving.

EMOTIONS

Kaphas are very loyal and extremely faithful. So when two Kaphas get together, they can feel comfortable that their partner will not stray.

However, they may have another problem. Kaphas can be possessive and greedy. When out of balance, they can feel insecure and want to keep those they love extremely close to them. They can also be "hoarders"—the people who collect things and can't seem to get enough. They don't want to let go of anything and end up with too much of it.

This applies to food, too. Kaphas tend to turn to food for comfort. When upset, they'll grab something sweet and hole up in their sanctuary and eat. What they really should do is just the opposite! They will feel much better, and more balanced, if they take off on their bikes for a while, or visit a spa for a stimulating massage.

If the Kapha couple can recognize these behaviors, they can help each other to stay in balance. Kaphas are generally very healthy people. They have good stamina and are resistant to illnesses. But they often take this for granted. When they take care of themselves, they can live a long and productive life.

A Word of Advice

Kaphas tend to be emotional eaters—the best thing that they can do for themselves is to keep active, keep moving!

SEX

When it comes to sex, Kaphas seek quality over quantity. They are very romantic and like to take their time. The Kaphas are eager to please each other and don't like to be rushed.

Kapha can maintain passion for the long haul, which is why

Kapha couples stay together for so many years. They enjoy sex, but they keep it in perspective. Kapha is cohesive; it holds things together. There is a lot of stability in their long-term partnership. They're more focused on their family in general.

Kaphas are very fertile and the Kapha couple tends to have many children. They both love kids, so the kids grow up feeling happy and cared for. Because of the genetics involved, Kapha mates tend to produce Kapha children, so the family tree can be very extensive.

Food

Food is Kapha's biggest weakness. Kaphas love food and love to eat. They especially love sweet foods, though those are the worst for them. One of the big reasons that sweets are so bad for Kaphas is that they tend to be higher calorie foods, and Kapha is prone to weight gain.

There are a few general rules that Kaphas can follow to keep their weight in check:

Basic Rules for the Kapha Diet

Look for foods that are bitter, spicy, and tangy.
Avoid foods that are sweet, sour, or salty.
Eat smaller portions.
Do not eat between meals.
Do not eat because of your emotional state, whether to celebrate or to soothe.
Walk after a meal, do not rest or sleep.
Drink fewer liquids during the meal, especially avoiding cold drinks.

Kapha partners can work together on their diet and exercise routines. It is easy for them to cook at home because they'll both be eating the same things. They can post this list of rules on the refrigerator and remind themselves of what it takes to stay in balance.

TRAVEL

The Kapha couple doesn't take many vacations—they've got such a great home that they're content to just hang out there when they have time off. But when they do travel, they prefer long, leisurely trips. They like to go on vacation to relax rather than to sightsee!

But too much relaxation leads to lethargy with Kapha, so this isn't always the best thing for them. One way to get around this is to go on an organized tour. This way, they won't have to worry about making reservations and arrangements; it will all be taken care of for them. And they are bound to have some "free" days when they can just do their own thing as well.

A cruise would be a wonderful vacation for this pair. The motion of the ship helps to stimulate Kapha, and there is a nice balance of activity and downtime. They just need to watch out for those "all-you-can-eat" buffets and remember that the food rules apply even when in foreign waters! Kaphas need to add spice to their lives and will enjoy dancing the night away to salsa or swing music.

Kaphas enjoy just about any climate, as long as it is not too humid or too cold.

Getaway

Kaphas would be happiest having a picnic in the mountains, under the pine trees, and a walk in the fresh air.

WORK

Kaphas are known for being really good with money and they make excellent accountants. You will also find many Kaphas in the field of medicine, because they are good nurturers and caretakers and have the patience and stamina that it takes to get through medical school. Perhaps the Kapha couple will meet in medical school, and they will both be doctors.

Kaphas are very dependable and make good managers. They can keep a business running smoothly. People trust Kaphas; they can be excellent negotiators. And because Kaphas are patient and thorough, they also make good mechanics and technicians.

Once the children arrive, both the Kapha man and Kapha woman will want to spend more time at home with the kids. Kaphas are not career-driven. Their goal is to save money so that they can retire early and spend more time at home. And they do this very well! Kaphas have a knack for saving money and often end up very wealthy.

Business

The Kapha couple does well with their own mom-and-pop store. Their store is their home away from home, and their customers feel welcome and well-served, and return again and again.

GREAT DATES

Kaphas don't need a lot of conversation, so they can go to a place where they are entertained and mentally stimulated. The theater is wonderful for Kaphas—whether it's a rousing comedy or a lively musical. They tend not to like heavy dramas, however, because they get depressed pretty easily. If they go to see a musical, they'll want to buy the soundtrack and sing along with the songs in the car on the way home. Kaphas have beautiful voices and harmonize well with each other.

Kaphas don't need to spend a lot of money on each other in the courting process. In fact, it is more appealing to them to be shown genuine personal gestures and know that the other person is as wise about money and finance as they are.

SENSUAL PLEASURES

Kaphas are wonderful kissers and they love kissing each other every chance they get. They're very affectionate with one another, even in public.

Aromatherapy works wonders for the Kapha couple, because they respond strongly to seductive scents. There are a lot of ways they can use aromatherapy, from scented massage oils to aroma pots to simmering spices on the stove.

Since good smells are a turn-on, it follows that bad smells are a turn-off. Personal care makes a big difference-scented creams and lotions go a long way in arousing the Kapha libido.

Massages are great for Kaphas, too. They can take turns with each other, using corn or olive oil, which are Kapha-balancing and readily available at the supermarket. Massages get the blood circulating and bring heat to the muscles. This is all good for a night of seduction.

AT HOME

A house full of Kaphas is a happy one. The Kapha mom is great about keeping track of family memories and will take photos at every occasion. She may even have scrapbooks set aside for each of the kids.

The family hangs out at home more often than they go out, so they spend money on making it a great place to be. They have a big-screen TV and a collection of DVDs, and they'll spend many evenings enjoying these together.

To help keep Kapha in balance, the couple should decorate with bright, bold colors. They particularly like warm colors: red, gold, and orange.

CIRCLE OF FRIENDS

Kaphas like to have people around then, whether it is family or friends. Their house may not be totally organized, but it is comfortable and cozy; guests truly are made to feel at home.

History carries a lot of weight with Kaphas, and most of the friends they have are ones that they have had for a very long time.

FAMILY DYNAMICS

Kaphas have such a large family, with aunts and uncles and cousins of every age, that it's a party every time they get together! Weddings are a big deal; so are birthdays and anniversaries—Kapha families remember the important occasions and love an excuse to celebrate.

Both the Kapha mom and the Kapha dad feel strongly about putting family first and will insist on the kids being home for family dinners. They will all attend church together (preferably the later service so that they can sleep in on the weekends). The kids may get away with a lot, because neither mom nor dad likes to be the disciplinarian. But when Dad's deep voice booms out in disapproval, the kids listen. He may not say much, but what he does say is important!

Kaphas are generally healthy and strong, but they are prone to allergies, which may run in the family.

12

MANTRA & TANTRA:

EXPRESSING YOURSELF
WITH YOUR MIND AND BODY

With passion pray.
With passion make love.
With passion eat and drink and dance and play.
—RUMI

MANTRA

The ancient Vedic texts explain that everything is made up of sound. Sound, or vibration, is the purest form of energy, and there is no doubt that sound can affect us profoundly. Our words carry weight. We can be moved by poetry and hurt by unkind comments. The music we listen to can uplift us or give us a headache. Thunder makes us shudder. The voice of a loved one provides reassurance.

Mantra means "instrument of the mind." Mantras are sounds made up of sacred Sanskrit syllables that, when put together, help us harness spiritual energy. Chanting mantras, or even just reciting them, gives us access to our creative spirit and brings harmony to our minds and bodies. Sounds can actually help us to activate our inner pharmacy and bring balance to our physiology, creating wellness and vitality.

Mantras are used for various purposes; there are many different ones you can use depending on exactly what you want to learn or manifest. Volumes have been written on this subject, and it is a fascinating study. But because we are talking about relationships in this book, let's look specifically at how mantras can help you attract a wonderful partner into your life.

What do you want?

In any endeavor, the results that we achieve are directly related to the quality of our intentions. We need to begin with a clear understanding of exactly what it is that we want. In the West, we tend to base our criteria for relationships on superficial values. For example, men seem to want women who look good, and women seem to want men with money. Are we really defining what would satisfy the soul? The Vedic texts have a different system for placing value on a relationship, one that is meant to help us grow spiritually as individuals and as couples.

Shiva & Shakti

According to Vedic literature, creation takes two energies. One energy is masculine, and it's called *Shiva*. The other energy is feminine, and it's called *Shakti*. In stories, they are portrayed as a god and goddess. Shiva represents consciousness and Shakti represents power. When Shiva and Shakti got together, they danced and the universe was created.

In this scenario, to create (and recreate and procreate!) men and women need each other. This balance of energy helps to make us whole, and we need to recognize the importance that both energies bring to the table. The Vedic tradition shows us that women empower men, that feminine energy is a giving force rather than a taking one.

When you are making your intentions clear about what you are looking for in a relationship, you need to keep this in mind. A man is indeed receiving a wonderful gift when a loving woman comes into his life and gives him her energy. This energy gives him power and helps him to reach his goals. A woman wants to find a man who will receive her energy in a positive way. She needs commitment and reciprocity. When the two share their energies they both become better people. They are transformed. This is what we are all searching for—real intimacy, a natural giving and receiving that works both ways.

The energies of Shiva and Shakti are not so much opposites as they are complementary. Just as we each have all three doshas in our composition, we each have masculine and feminine energies within us as well. It is the union of these two energies that allows us unlimited potential.

INTIMACY

There are two ingredients that make up true intimacy. The first one is time. The process of courtship is important. This is the getting-to-know-you phase. When we take the time to learn about the person we are with, we also learn about ourselves and what we can contribute to a healthy relationship. The second ingredient is truth. Truthfulness is the foundation from which a relationship can grow. We need to be honest in every way, and about every thing. Without truth there can be no intimacy. Truth starts with being honest with ourselves.

MAGNETIC ATTRACTION

Using a mantra helps both to awaken and to bring into balance the Shiva and Shakti within you. At the same time, the mantra strengthens your power of attraction and turns you into a magnet— people will be drawn to you. This is another reason why you need to have a clear understanding of what you want. Your intention can't merely be to attract "some rich guy" or "some beautiful girl." When you are seeking your life partner, you are seeking someone who will respect and honor your energy and who will give his or her energy for your benefit in return. And you are seeking truth. From truth comes all those other great things that make a relationship last, including trust. So it is important to be clear not only in the words you say, but in the thoughts you think as well.

Here is the mantra to use when a woman seeks a man:

Sat Patim Dehi
This is pronounced: Saht Pah-teem Day-hee.
It translates to "Please bring me a man of truth and goodness."

Here is the mantra to use when a man seeks a woman:

Patneem Manoramam Dehi
This is pronounced: Paht-neem Mah-nor-a-mahm Day-hee.
It translates to "Please bring me a woman of truth and beauty."

The effectiveness of the mantra is determined by how much devotion and concentration is behind it. Like everything else in life, you'll get out of it what you put into it. If you are serious about your search and have strong intentions, you will want to put effort into this task. If you are a man seeking a man, or a woman seeking a woman, you may use the same mantras. Remember that in Ayurveda, the essence of male or female is in the energy, so you are looking to balance someone else's energy with your own.

The Mantra Ritual

Although you can repeat your mantra anywhere, at any time of day, it is nice to set a special time aside just for the ritual of the mantra. Before beginning your practice, wash your hands, as this symbolizes purity. Imagine that the impurities of your mind are being washed away. Find a comfortable place where you can be quiet and undisturbed for a while. If it will help you get in the mood, you may choose to sit facing the east, to light a candle, and/or to sit in a cross-legged position. Close your eyes, and concentrate on each syllable of the mantra. Mantras may be repeated either silently or out loud. Continue repeating the mantra over and over again. The repetition will bring you a deep sense of peace and joy. When you feel you are done, sit quietly for a moment and give thanks to the Siddhas, the sages of ancient India, for their wisdom and generosity in passing these mantras on for you to use. Then slowly open your eyes, take a few breaths, and go on with your usual activity.

MALA BEADS

A tool that may help to focus the mind, and is often used in Vedic tradition, is the *mala*. A mala is very much like a rosary: It helps us to "count" our mantras. It is a string of 108 beads. Some malas have 54 beads, in which case you use the mala to do two "rounds" of mantras. The number 108 is significant on many levels. It is representative of the nine planets, multiplied by the twelve astrological signs. One hundred and eight is also a holy number the numeral 1, written as a vertical line, symbolizes God, or the Supreme Energy from which all other lines begin. Zero represents a circle (0), showing that God's creation is complete and perfect. And 8, when seen on its side (∞), is the mathematical sign for infinity, or eternity, reminding us that creation goes on eternally. In numerology, 108 adds up to the number 9, which is the number of completeness and wholeness.

The chain of beads represents life as an endless chain of events, of cause and effect. The mala is tied together with a special bead called "Mount Meru." When you reach this bead, the mala is to be turned and the movement continued in the other direction. Mount Meru symbolizes that we can rise above our perceived limitations. The mala is often held at heart level, which emphasizes the devotional aspect of the mantra ritual.

Using a mala gives your hands something to do, which helps to release nervous energy. It's a way of bringing the mind and body together to focus your thought. If you're interested in trying it, here's how it works: Roll each bead, one at a time, between your thumb and your ring finger. Repeat the mantra, and move on to the next bead. Mala beads are very personal, because they take on some of your energy as you use them. You may wear your mala beads as a necklace, with the Mount Meru in front, or as a bracelet, wrapped around your wrist. Wearing this mala is supposed to remind you of your mantra and your clear intention. At night, place your mala under your pillow while you sleep or on your altar (if you have one).

REMINDERS

Another way to keep this mantra in your mind is to post it wherever you might see it during the day. You can hang little notes to yourself on the bathroom mirror, on the refrigerator door, near the phone, on the computer, or even on the dashboard of your car. You can repeat the mantra as you're walking through the grocery store, or working out at the gym.

MORE MANTRAS

If you're in a relationship and want it to grow stronger, there's a mantra for that, too! This mantra helps to heal relationships by bringing you clarity of thought:

Om Nama Shivaya
This is pronounced: Ohm Nah-mah Shee-vah-yah
Translated, it means: "I honor the Divine within."

The mantra is meant to remind you of the light within yourself and within every one of us. Used over time, it helps you to grow spiritually to our highest potential. You can use this mantra specifically for that purpose, too.

Another well-known mantra for spiritual growth is this:

Om Mani Padme Hum
This is pronounced: Ohm Mah-nee Pahd-may Hoom.
Translated, it means: "I surrender to the jewel (or pearl) within the lotus."

It is repeated to remind you of your commitment to your spiritual advancement. It embraces the world with love. The lotus is a frequent symbol in Vedic philosophy. It is a beautiful flower with many layers; it opens up to the light, and it grows out of the mud and sludge at the bottom of a body of water. This represents how beautiful you are, regardless of your background or origin, and how you can unfold and grow when you reach for the light.

This is a mantra to use to bless food, as "grace" before a meal:

Om Annapurnayai Namaha
This is pronounced: Ohm Ah-nah-poor-nah-yai Nah-mah-hah
Translated, this means: "We give thanks to Annapurna, the Goddess of food."

This is a mantra to use for world peace, or even peace at home:

Om Shanti Shanti Shanti
This is pronounced: Ohm Shahn-tee Shahn-tee Shahn-tee
Translated, this means: "Peace, peace, peace, let there be peace."

Mantras for the Doshas

DOSHA	MANTRA	PRONUNCIATION	PURPOSE
Vata	Ram	Rahm	helps boost immune system, alleviates fear and anxiety
Pitta	Shrim	Shreem	promotes general health and harmony
Kapha	Hum	Hoom	clearing, stimulating

TANTRA

Tantra means "instrument of the body" and also "technique." Tantra sounds exotic, but it is actually very simple, and the basic principles of Tantra help us to see the beauty in all aspects of life.

Tantra is about optimizing the energy that is created when the masculine and feminine come together. It teaches us about using our bodies to become conscious of pleasure. And it is about evolving and finding more joy and ecstasy in our lives by being present to reality.

THE FIVE SENSES

Tantra teaches us to use all five of our senses consciously. Sounds easy enough, but how often do we really do that? We tend to go through our experiences with a kind of apathy, a been-there, done-that kind of attitude. Stop it! Our senses allow us to get in touch with the physical and are a gateway to great pleasure, sensual pleasure.

Sparsa

Sparsa means "touch" in Sanskrit. The skin marks the visible limits of the body, and it is at the boundaries of the skin where we make contact with the world. Our skin is our largest organ. It is 16 percent of our body weight and covers about 15 square feet of area. When we "feel" something emotionally, we say, "it touched me." When we are born, it is touch that wakes up our system. With touch we experience much of our environment: the temperature, our clothes, our sheets, a shower.

Our skin has a kind of three-dimensional perception. We feel touch, temperature, and pressure. We have different kinds of skin on our bodies that vary in texture and thickness, such as our lips, our eyelids, the soles of our feet, our elbows. Notice the differences, and see how they are all connected, how it is all part of one.

Here's an exercise you can do with your partner to wake up your sense of sparsa:

Collect several items made of different materials and textures, such as a feather, a velvet hat, baby powder, a silk scarf, or a peach. Next, take turns: Have your partner lay down on the bed, wearing minimal clothing to expose a maximum amount of skin. Ask your partner to close his or her eyes, or if he or she is comfortable with the idea, have you partner wear a blindfold. Gently stroke the skin with one of the items, taking your time and allowing the person to really experience that item, its texture and temperature. Ask your partner to concentrate on the feeling, and the emotions and associations that come up. You may want to play a guessing game, and figure out a prize for how many items are guessed correctly. And make sure to take turns!

Sabda

Sabda is the Sanskrit word for "sound." As I discussed in the mantra section of this chapter, sounds have a profound effect on the body. Studies have shown that sounds can open up our inner pharmacy and balance our physiology. In other words, they can help us be healthier! Experiment with different sounds and observe how each one makes you feel. You might want to crank up some lively music and allow your body the freedom to dance with abandon around the room. Experience how the vibrations of different musical instruments resonate in your body. Try pounding a drum, and just go with the flow, hear whatever beat starts coming out spontaneously. Sit near a low-pitched gong, or a high-pitched bell. Go to the beach and listen to the ocean waves. How does your body respond to those various tones?

Rasa

Rasa means "taste." The tongue is super-sensitive. With any of these exercises, it helps to isolate the one sense by blocking out the others when possible. So again, you might close your eyes or use a blindfold to experience rasa more fully. Savor and delight in the tastes and textures of various foods and drinks, such as whipped cream, chocolate, a peppermint stick, an ice cube, a strawberry, a dill pickle, a maraschino cherry, a lemon wedge, or a pretzel. You can use what you have on hand or prepare for the experience by shopping for some out-of-the-ordinary indulgences ahead of time.

Gandha

Gandha means "smell." Women are particularly sensitive to smells, as are all Kaphas. Our pheromones are the scents that we give off without even realizing it. These pheromones train us to recognize and desire our partners. When people stop smoking, they say that they rediscover their sense of smell. Studies have shown that the loss of the olfactory sense is often accompanied by a loss in sexual interest, so it is a good idea to keep our noses functioning optimally! Fragrances have quite an allure to them. An entire industry is built around perfume, for example. We covet that "new car smell." We know the sweet smell of a newborn baby. The smell of coffee brewing (decaf, of course!) is warm and inviting. Go through an exercise with your partner to identify different aromas, and see which ones set off different sensations in your body.

Rupa

Rupa in Sanskrit means "sight." We rely on our sense of sight so much, and yet it is probably the sense we take most for granted. To open your eyes to different things, you need to change your point of view! Get away from the computer screen for a while and take a walk in nature. Notice the clouds in the sky and find shapes in them, the way you did when you were a kid. Find grass that's somehow managed to poke its way through cracks in the cold hard cement. Visit a museum and visually take in the beauty that talented artists have created. People-watch and recognize the beauty in and around each individual.

BREATHE

Tantra recognizes that our breath is what gives us life. We can breathe "consciously" by becoming aware of our breath. Take long, slow breaths from your diaphragm. Pay attention to both the inhale and the exhale. Conscious breathing benefits us by

✦ decreasing stress
✦ helping to develop sensory sensitivity
✦ improving sleep
✦ calming the body and mind
✦ improving mental capacity and concentration
✦ generating feelings of fulfillment and joy

Try this exercise with your partner to help bring you closer together:

1. Sit on the bed or on the floor and face each other. Get as close as you can.
2. Look into each other's eyes.
3. Breathe together, develop a rhythm so that you are inhaling and exhaling in unison. Do this for a few minutes without speaking, just looking at each other and breathing.
4. Then, while still looking into each other's eyes, start practicing "shared" breathing. While one inhales, the other exhales, and vice versa. Do this for a few minutes.

You'll find that you are drawn closer and closer together as you synchronize your breaths.

AWARENESS

Tantra teaches us to pay attention to life. Rather than always thinking about all the things you desire, pretend for a moment that everything desires you! You are in this world, a part of this world, and everything is here to be with you. The floor you walk on loves feeling your footsteps. The trees fill with leaves so that you will sit in the shade beneath their branches. The cup you hold yearns for your lips. It is a different experience when your mouth touches an object that desires you! You can carry this experience over into your relationship. Be aware of your partner. Feel the desire.

THE TEMPLE

Tantra explains that bliss cannot exist without the body, just as fragrance cannot exist without the flower. See your body as a temple. See your body as beautiful and pure. Be grateful for this body and for the bliss you are free to experience because of it.

13

Sons & Daughters:
How the Doshas Can Help You Parent

You that come to birth and bring the mysteries,
your voice-thunder makes us very happy.
—RUMI

BEFORE WE WERE men and women, we were boys and girls. In general, our constitutions don't change much. When we are in balance, we have the same proportion of Vata, Pitta, and Kapha that we were born with.

However, just as each season has its own dosha, each age has its own dosha, and we are more susceptible to that particular dosha's influence at that time in our lives.

Knowledge of the doshas and their attributes can be very useful to us when it comes to parenting. When we understand our children's strengths, we can help them develop their natural talents and abilities. Awareness of the doshas also helps us learn to communicate more easily, and to be more accepting and loving people. So when our children look to us to see how to act and see that we take care of ourselves and have respect for other human beings, our kids will act accordingly. But first, let's look at how the doshas affect the phases of our lives in a general sense.

KAPHA

Childhood has all the qualities of Kapha. This season of our lives lasts from the moment we are born until about age twenty. As children, we are more Kapha-like. We may have a little bit of baby fat and we're more calm and carefree. We place an emphasis on friendship and love to be cuddled.

Children go through a stage where they are very possessive. They identify things as "mine!" They don't want to share. They hoard their toys and start collections. These are Kapha traits. As parents and teachers, we understand that this is a part of their growth process and gently teach them how to get along with others and how to relate better to other people. We need to remember these lessons as adults in the world.

When we are children, it might take longer for us to learn things, but once we learn them, we never forget. It might have taken quite a while to learn the alphabet, to get all twenty-six letters in the right order, but I think most of us have got it down now, even though we don't practice every day!

When we're very young, we take a lot of naps and sleep many hours at a time. Then we go through another stage as teenagers where we sleep a lot, too. This is very Kapha-like behavior.

Kids also tend to get a lot of colds, especially during the preschool years. Colds and congestion are Kapha imbalances. Like increases like, and kids share their germs freely when they gather together on a regular basis. Kapha associated with Kapha produces more Kapha, and too much Kapha leads to imbalance. Getting kids on a Kapha routine during these times will help to balance them out.

PITTA

Sometime around age twenty our Pitta nature starts to kick in. We might be in college, or just entering the workforce, and our ambition becomes important to us. We become more competitive;

we want to get ahead. We start thinking about money and wanting luxury items like nice clothes or fast cars.

At this age, we are very busy building our careers and are very work-oriented. This is the thinking and planning phase of our lives. We've got this fire burning inside us, so we're a little more aggressive when going after what we want. We can be impatient.

We use our intellect more during this time than any other. Whether we're studying for exams or learning about our chosen field on the job, we are constantly thinking. We're also strategizing and positioning ourselves. We analyze where we are and where we're going. We like being in control.

As a part of this planning stage, we're also looking for our lifetime partners. We're discerning in this process, sorting out our priorities. We have lots of choices to make, but we know what we want—or at least we think we do! Our sexual desire is at its peak.

This is also the time when we are raising our families and establishing our homes. We are making decisions about neighborhoods and schools, and watching where we spend our money.

VATA

At about age forty, Vata comes strongly into play and we become more Vata-like as we grow older. We start noticing that we don't remember things as well. There's a joke that circulated around the Internet about "Age-Activated Attention Deficit Disorder." Attention deficit disorder is actually a Vata imbalance, so there is a lot of truth in the humor. At this age, our attention is divided among work, family, community, and other responsibilities, so we naturally have more on our minds. I don't know who started it, but it goes something this:

> "It looks like there is finally a diagnosis for my condition: A.A.A.D.D.: Age-Activated Attention Deficit Disorder. The symptoms? Let's look at a typical day. First I decide to go to the market. Where did I put that grocery list? Oh, over here by the mail. I put down my car keys and as I'm throwing out

the junk mail I notice the garbage can needs to be emptied. So, I put the bills on the table and then I'll empty the can. But since I'm going out, I'll get a few bills into the mailbox on my way.

But first I've got to find my checkbook, which is in my purse, which is . . . got it! Except I'm out of checks. Back to the desk, and on my way I'll put those dirty dishes in the dishwasher—which needs to be unloaded first. So, I'll stack them in the sink for now. What is the cat doing in the sink? Now she's all wet, I've got to dry her off. No towel on the rack? I'll use the potholder, then throw it in the laundry room. As I head back to the kitchen I'm thinking—now what was it I was going to do?

At the end of the day, I haven't gotten the groceries, the bills haven't been paid, there is cat hair in the sink, I'm out of checks, and I can't find my car keys! But I can't figure out how nothing got done today, because I know I was busy all day long! Yes, this is a serious condition, and I will seek help. But first I think I'll check my e-mail."

As we get older, more of Vata's physical ailments present themselves, too. Our fertility decreases. We may begin to have digestive problems, and our hearing may get a little worse. All these things are the effects of more Vata present in our system. This is the time for us to adapt our diet and exercise programs to include more Vata foods and activities.

Sometime after age sixty we may become more Kapha-like again. We slow down and want to surround ourselves with family. We're more concerned with comfort. It may be more difficult to stimulate ourselves physically to keep in balance, but we can certainly stimulate ourselves mentally, by taking classes and learning new things. We can continue to do things that we enjoy and engage in conversations with people we respect.

	VATA	PITTA	KAPHA
Learns best by	listening	reading, visuals	association
Memory	learns quickly, forgets quickly	good, sharp memory	learns slowly, but then doesn't forget

PARENTING

Parenting is an application of love in our daily lives. Our children give us the opportunity to experience and express love every day. As parents, we have a very unique relationship with each of our children. We interact with them on so many different levels at the same time. We can be a teacher, friend, chauffeur, psychologist, advisor, disciplinarian, coach, referee, and more! When you know your child's dominant dosha, you are better able to handle the myriad of things that come up in any given moment. You are better able to parent from a place of love rather than expectation. You know, for example, that your Vata child may have some anxiety about a friend's sleepover. Or that your Kapha child may need two alarm clocks to get up in the morning.

Mind-body type does have genetic components. But a family isn't necessarily dominant in one dosha or another. A Kapha mother and father very well could have a Pitta child, for example. You need to look on both sides of the family to see from where a dosha was inherited. For example, a Pitta child could get her blue eyes from her mother's Pitta mother, or her athletic ability from her father's Pitta brother.

It is interesting to look back at your own childhood and discover the doshas of each of your brothers and sisters. Look at how you interacted with your siblings. What were these relationships like? Remember that your kids look to you for skills to handle each other, too. They learn from your example.

KAPHA KIDS

Kapha kids tend to be more solidly built. They're stockier and more resistant to illness. They love to eat and have a sweet tooth. You need to watch their diets so that they don't overeat. Kapha children are very caring. They'll be the first ones to give you a hug. They may be a little shy at first, but once they warm up, they're all smiles.

Kapha kids like to lounge around, so make sure there are plenty of activities for them to participate in so that they don't turn into couch potatoes. If given a choice, the Kapha child would choose playing video games over a trampoline, but the trampoline would do so much more to keep him or her in balance. To get Kapha kids outdoors, have them help in the garden—they love tending to flowers and gardening.

Kaphas tend to have beautiful singing voices, so it's a good idea to nurture that at a young age. Have your kids join the church choir, or take singing lessons.

In school, it seems like Kapha kids take longer to learn things, but the positive side to this is that once they learn something, they don't forget it. Kaphas learn best by association, so it's a good idea to tell stories and give them experiences that help make the subject matter relevant to them. Be patient with them, work at their speed, and don't give up.

Kapha kids tend to be very loyal and loving toward their friends, but they are also sensitive and their feelings are easily hurt.

Kapha Girls

Kapha girls have big, beautiful eyes and thick, wavy hair. They love to play house and have lots of dolls. They can be very popular when they're younger because they laugh at everyone's jokes and love to be around other kids. It seems like they're always in love with someone. But as they get older, they may get picked on if they have weight problems. It's a challenge to teach girls self-esteem once they get into middle school, so it is important to instill this in them from the very beginning. Give them lots of praise and encouragement, and teach them Kapha-balancing habits that they can use throughout their lives.

Kapha Boys

The Kapha boys may be the plump, cute kids in elementary school, but with activity and exercise, they can grow up to be the star football players in high school! They're also the wrestlers and water-polo players. Weight lifting and other stimulating exercises, such as running, are great for balancing Kapha, and if they can get into these habits early it will help them all along the way. You can often tell a Kapha boy by his bushy eyebrows and thick lashes.

PITTA KIDS

Pitta kids are the ones who play baseball, basketball, soccer, and hockey. They go from one sport to the next and like best whichever one they're doing at the time! The Pitta kid wants to be the best one on the team and wants to bring home the trophy to prove it.

Sometimes, if you're lucky, the Pitta competitive spirit will spill over into the classroom. The Pitta child will be motivated to work hard and get good grades. He or she will be keenly aware of grade point average and do extra-credit work (if necessary) to make honor roll. Pitta kids are great at memorizing and do well with flash cards, which is a visual tool for learning. They love to read.

Pittas can be show-offy, and they like to be in charge. As parents you can teach them social skills to help them control their anger and get along with everyone.

Pitta Girls

Pitta girls want to run the show. They'll seek office in the student council with the platform that they can "get things done!" And they can do just that, as long as they don't get caught up in their perfectionism. Sometimes they'd rather not do something at all rather than risk doing it less than perfectly. This is a big burden to carry and can stress out a kid no end.

The overachievers at school are often the Pitta girls, but because they are so critical, they can also be the bullies. They want things their way, meaning that kids who don't comply with their rules are picked on or excluded. Make sure that your Pitta girl learns what it means to work as a part of the team, rather than always having the leadership position.

Pitta Boys

These are the jocks, the "fair-haired" boys who always seem to have everything so easy. Maybe people assume these boys have it easy because they have a lot of confidence. They are well-spoken, articulate and make fine leaders. But inside, they can be frustrated. They expect a lot from themselves, and may even be feeling pressured by their Pitta parents. A Pitta-balancing routine will help them to be their best, and feel their best, inside and out.

VATA KIDS

The daydreamy child drawing rainbows on a pad in the back of the room is the Vata child. These kids have great imaginations, and they're gifted at making up stories. If you ask them a question, they'll talk up a storm. They're often perceived as "spacey" or "weird."

Physically, Vata is slight. Whether tall or short, these kids look skinny; they have narrow hips and shoulders. Their appetite varies, but no matter how much they eat, they don't seem to put on weight.

Vata kids learn things quickly, but then they forget them almost as quickly. You might think they've got their times tables down cold, only to have them fail a test the next day. Very often, kids with attention deficit/hyperactivity disorder are Vata dominant. They are auditory learners, so sometimes it's easier for them to listen to a book-on-tape rather than try to sit still and read for long periods of time. A multimodal approach to learning in general is best for Vata kids—they like to hear it, see it, touch it, and experience it.

They're great at all things creative and likely will be in the school plays, draw cartoons for the school paper, or be nominated for class clown.

Lots of hugs and a warm environment help keep Vata kids from getting out of balance and feeling nervous.

Vata Girls

Make sure you always have lots of paper and colored pens and pencils on hand when you have a Vata girl. They need an outlet for their creativity and you want to make sure that all their energy is directed in positive ways. Vata girls love writing in diaries. They'll fill up blank book after blank book with poems and sketches and all their childhood experiences. How wonderful for them to save these books and look back as their talents blossom! Vata girls are drama queens. You can find them in any school's theater department. And they're not only acting in the plays, they're writing the scripts, designing the costumes, and painting the sets. A Vata-balancing lifestyle will help these girls stay in balance and keep them from burning themselves out.

Vata Boys

You'll find Vata boys in the computer room, lost in the world of high-tech potential. They'll also be in the bookstore, looking for another Ray Bradbury novel or flipping through the texts on animation and *The Simpsons*. These are the class clowns, the ones who make up the kookiest stories, who get into trouble but can talk their way out of it. Vata boys are fun to be around, but it's a challenge to keep them tuned in to this universe and focused on the task at hand. Helping them understand and incorporate the Vata routine will bring balance and calm to their lives.

GROWING AND GLOWING

It doesn't matter how many children you have; as a parent you soon learn that you can't parent any two kids the same way. When we look at all the factors involved in a child's individuality and the different ages and stages they all go through, there is no question that parenting is the most difficult job there is! Ayurveda gives us tools to help us relate to our children, and to help our children relate to each other.

14

Friends & Associates:
You Can Get Along with Anyone

Tonight, a singing competition:
Jupiter, the moon, and myself,
the friends I've been looking for!
—RUMI

IN ANY SETTING with many different types of people, it is interesting to observe the interactions that go on. We learn so much about ourselves by looking at the way we relate to people and they relate to us. Wherever people are thrown together, by choice or happenstance, a little "society" emerges, and everyone plays his or her role.

Ever notice how you just naturally "click" with some people, whereas with others it's a bit of a struggle? When you start looking at things the Vedic way, you begin to understand that there really are no coincidences, no accidents. All of the people in your life are there for a reason. And whatever the reason turns out to be, you will learn and grow from the experience. Sometimes you learn the most from the situations that bring you the most challenges. It may not always be fun, but it is always worthwhile!

By looking at the doshas, we can discover ways that we can help each other, by bringing our strengths and gifts to any given situation.

We can enhance our personal lives and our work lives by recognizing and appreciating the good that can come from all kinds of everyday human interaction.

WORK

Vata

Freelancers and others who work independently are often Vata types. Vatas like to do their own thing, and they don't like to keep to a set schedule. They are happy when they can make their own hours. When the spirit strikes them, Vatas work really hard and get a lot accomplished. But when they're not in the mood for work, they are easily distracted and unproductive. Hopefully, this all balances out and the Vata person is disciplined enough to get everything done that needs to be done.

In most office settings, there will be a nice representation of all three doshas. Here, the Vatas are in the creative areas. They're in the art department, or in promotions, or development. They can dream up new ideas, decorate the office, or write press releases.

When Vatas get excited about a project, the whole building will know it! Their energy level is high, even hyperactive, and their enthusiasm spills over into other areas. Don't be surprised if the project goes over budget. Vata is not one to pinch pennies.

Vata is great at starting projects but has difficulty following through. Vatas tend to get bored easily, and if they run into too many tiresome obstacles, their attention will focus on the newest and shiniest thing out there. What to do? Put some Pittas and Kaphas on their team!

Pitta

Pittas make great leaders. They're really good at planning and they pay attention to details. Pitta thinks logically and won't let Vata get carried away with elaborate extravagances. Pittas are also good at articulating what needs to be done and delegating the work fairly. Pittas are results-oriented, so they'll make sure that the project is completed and that it is done well.

Pittas make excellent lawyers. They're good at making their points and they like the challenge of debating someone head-on. Put a Pitta in the business affairs department of a company and let him or her sort out the fine print—Pittas excel in this area!

On a movie set, the director is most likely a Pitta. A director has to have a detailed schedule and know everything that is going on. He or she has to be able to negotiate with people and solve problems on the spot. Ron Howard, the acclaimed director, is a good example of a Pitta. Pittas are great at multitasking and directors do a lot of that. (His reddish hair is also a dead giveaway!)

Pitta likes to be in control, and when things aren't going the way they want them to, Pittas can become impatient and angry. Hopefully, the Kaphas who are around will be a calming influence!

Kapha

Kaphas make good accountants; they'll make sure that the project does not go over budget. In fact, you'll probably have some money left over for a staff party, with Kapha in charge of the books! Kaphas are dependable. They rarely call in sick and are extremely loyal to their companies. Kaphas are the ones with the big retirement accounts, who started saving the day they started working.

Kaphas prefer to focus on one thing at a time. They like to see a project through to its completion. When you want to make sure something gets finished, give it to a Kapha to do.

Kaphas are caring, nurturing people who love children and animals. You'll find Kaphas working in hospitals, schools, and animal parks. At times, Kaphas can be lazy, so it's up to the Vatas around to stir up the energy and get Kapha going again!

FRIENDSHIPS

Vata

Vatas make fun friends. They're unpredictable and always up to something new and different. They love music and love to go out and listen to bands or go dancing.

Vatas have lots of friends, but very few close ones. They make friends easily, but they are so busy doing all their "stuff" that they don't always keep their friends for long. But if you meet Vata again after a long time has gone by, it will feel like you just saw each other yesterday. You'll tap into that wonderful Vata energy and pick up right where you left off!

Vatas are pretty much loners. They're not good leaders or followers; they just like to do their own thing. They're also not materialistic. They can make a lot of money, but they'll spend it just as fast.

Pitta

Pittas make most of their friends at work, because that's where they spend most of their time. They'll also have groups of friends in other social settings. For example, they might join a club or community group, or play a league sport.

Pittas are competitive, and they may try to one-up you all the time. They don't even realize that they're doing this, but they can't help it. Pittas get jealous pretty easily, too, so keep that in mind when you drive up to your friend's house in your new Jaguar convertible!

Pittas are loyal friends, but they make bitter enemies. You don't want to get on their bad side! They're intellectual, and not at all sentimental. They have clarity and can see different points of view. They think with their heads rather than their hearts.

Kapha

Kaphas make very loyal, long-term friends. They're the ones you can count on to bring you chicken soup when you catch a cold. They're the ones you can turn to when you need a few bucks to get out of a bind. They love to take care of their friends, and they love to feel needed. They place a huge value on friendship, and acknowledge everything that you do for them. Sometimes they can go a little overboard; when Kaphas are out of balance they can be clingy and possessive, or lustful and greedy.

Kaphas are emotional and sentimental. They're in love with love and are very romantic.

Kaphas are the kind of friends who like to sit around and watch the game. Pittas would rather be playing the game; Vatas would rather be creating a new game!

Take a look at these friendship pairs—they could be male-female pairs or two men and two women:

Vata & Vata

These two can have a lot of fun together. They play off of each other's imaginations and laugh like crazy. You might find them at a comedy club, or the Ripley's "Believe It or Not" museum. When they work on a project together, it can end up turning into something totally wacky and outrageous because they keep giving the other interesting ideas.

Vatas make good friends for each other because they both understand the Vata need for space. They can go for periods of time without seeing or hearing from one another and know that the friendship is still intact. Vatas can be loners, and they like it when they find someone who understands this and thinks it's just fine.

At the same time, Vata friends must make sure that they don't feed off of each other when they are out of balance. When one Vata is experiencing anxiety, the other needs to shore him or her up with reassurances, rather than getting caught up in the anxiety and making it worse. Things like anxiety can be contagious, so watch out!

Vata & Pitta

These two can go far when they team up. Vata generates the ideas and Pitta takes those ideas and comes up with a practical plan for implementing them. If Vata gets too spacey, Pitta brings Vata down to earth with reason and consistency. And when Pitta gets overworked and angry, Vata can lighten the mood and make Pitta laugh. If Pitta is competitive, it doesn't bother Vata, who is busy with other priorities.

Pitta just has to learn to be patient with what are perceived to be Vata's antics. And Vata needs to make sure that Pitta's fire is not stoked too often.

Vata & Kapha

Laurel and Hardy or Abbot and Costello come to mind with this pair. Those characters are extreme, but they illustrate pretty clearly the Vata and Kapha personas. They make good friends, because Vata gets Kapha going and Kapha slows Vata down—they balance each other out! As long as they both see that this is good for them, and it doesn't become a tug-of-war, then all is blissful.

Vata's get-up-and-go attitude introduces Kapha to lots of experiences that he or she otherwise wouldn't experience. And Kapha's laid-back attitude helps Vata to appreciate beauty by taking time to smell the roses.

There are times when Vata gets tired of having to be the ringleader and leaves Kapha behind for a while. And there are times when Kapha is worn out by Vata's excessive energy and chooses to remain behind. But the friendship endures, because Kapha is so loyal and Vata is happy to have someone to rely on. Vata is a good talker, and Kapha is a good listener.

Pitta & Pitta

It's better if these two are teammates rather than on opposite sides. They are super-competitive, and if they are up against each other, it could carry over into the friendship. They will fight tooth and nail in a debate, so imagine how heated their arguments can be.

On the plus side, Pittas are very organized and appreciate this about each other. They make great roommates because they respect order and routine and will follow the rules of the house. Pittas like to get things done, so when two of them team up, a lot can be accomplished. They just have to make sure that they both understand that they are on equal footing, because each prefers the leadership role. These are the kinds of friends that need to take turns driving!

Pitta & Kapha

Kapha tends to soften Pitta's sharp edges, and Pitta's warmth tends to bring out Kapha's affectionate nature. These two make good business partners: Kapha provides the stability and follow-through necessary for Pitta's plans to work, and Pitta lights a fire under Kapha to help get things started.

Kapha & Kapha

You might find these two at the movies feeding their sweet tooths with one of those oversized candy bars. But if so, it's probably a matinee, where they can get a discount, and they've most likely smuggled in some candy of their own because they'd rather not spend the money! Because they have this frugality in common, they don't mind just hanging out at home rather than going somewhere that costs big bucks.

Kaphas take their time getting to know each other, but when Kaphas make friends, they are friends for life. They both hold on to something as precious to them as friendship.

It would be nice if Kaphas could inspire each other and go work out or run together, but what happens more often is that they end up indulging themselves in food and comfort, because it's just so much easier!

All Together Now!

When you all go out to the movies, Kapha will be munching on popcorn. Pitta will have made all the arrangements—which theater, what time, who drives. Vata will be guessing what's going to happen next and coming up with the best lines. After the movie, Kapha will stretch and yawn. Pitta will analyze how long the movie was compared to the last one you saw and start planning for the following weekend. Vata will go on and on about the screenplay and cinematography and who should be up for awards.

When you're on a walk around the neighborhood and you come across a snake in the street, Vata will scream and run away. Pitta will go into attack mode and figure out how to best trap the critter. Kapha will keep walking and say, "Oh, a snake."

When it's time to celebrate birthdays, Kapha will want a nice party at home with friends and food. Pitta will want organized games and prizes. Vata will want to fly to Tibet and ride a camel.

Whenever possible, it is good to surround ourselves with people who are truthful and loving. In Sanskrit, such a gathering is called *satsanga*—it is uplifting and healing to our spirits to be in such company where everyone supports each other and wants the best for each other.

15

HOUSE & HOME:

CREATING A HAVEN FOR YOURSELF AND YOUR LOVED ONES

The universe is not outside of you.
Look inside yourself;
everything that you want,
you are already that.
—RUMI

JUST AS WE have relationships with other people, we also have a relationship with our environment. We are all connected to each other and to the universe. Our environments are an extension of ourselves, and we feel better and function more efficiently when we are in harmony with our environment. When your house is in order, the "outer" part of yourself, then you can focus your attention on your inner world. The spiritual journey really is an exploration of both the inner and the outer.

Ayurveda comes from the Vedic texts of India. In this same philosophy, there is a "science of architecture" known as *vastu*. The word *vastu* means, in its most basic sense, "a dwelling or site." Vastu is a blend of science and spirituality that gives us guidelines for enhancing our environments so we can create a space where we can live and work happily and productively. When we are happy with where we spend our time, our relationships with the people we spend our time with will be better, too!

Vastu has actually been around a lot longer than feng shui and is believed to be the inspiration for it. There are many similarities between the two. An in-depth discussion of vastu would be another book entirely, so I will just offer some guidelines as an introduction to this design system. If you would like more information, I recommend reading Kathleen Cox's book *Vastu Living: Creating a Home for the Soul.*

Both Ayurveda and vastu are based on the idea that the five elements (air, space, fire, water, and earth) are within us and all around us. In Vedic symbolism, the square represents the cosmos; it is the perfect form. Vastu looks at our living space as a square, and uses a compass to label each corner and the center with one of the five elements.

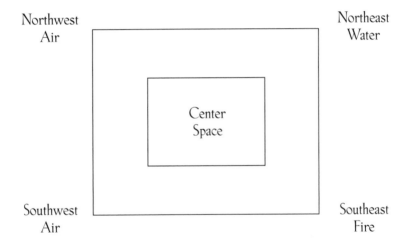

Northwest
Air

Northeast
Water

Center
Space

Southwest
Air

Southeast
Fire

In Ayurveda, the rule is that like increases like. So Vatas, who are predominantly composed of air and space, would not want to spend too much time in the northwest corner or center of their office or home, because that would increase their Vata and cause them to go out of balance. So the northwest area of Vata's living space would not be a good place his or her bedroom, for example.

Pittas, composed of more fire and water, would not want to spend too much time in the southeast or northeast corners.

Kaphas, composed mainly of earth and water, would not want to spend too much time in the northeast or southwest corners.

Just as in feng shui, the house itself has an orientation, and each room has its own orientation. Consult the following table to see where each room should be in the house, and then where each area should be within the room.

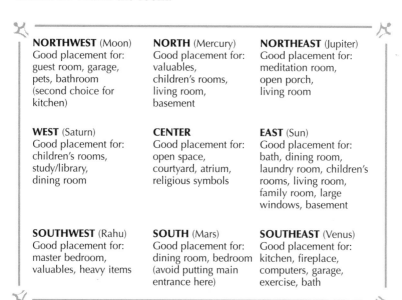

NORTHWEST (Moon)
Good placement for:
guest room, garage,
pets, bathroom
(second choice for
kitchen)

NORTH (Mercury)
Good placement for:
valuables,
children's rooms,
living room,
basement

NORTHEAST (Jupiter)
Good placement for:
meditation room,
open porch,
living room

WEST (Saturn)
Good placement for:
children's rooms,
study/library,
dining room

CENTER
Good placement for:
open space,
courtyard, atrium,
religious symbols

EAST (Sun)
Good placement for:
bath, dining room,
laundry room, children's
rooms, living room,
family room, large
windows, basement

SOUTHWEST (Rahu)
Good placement for:
master bedroom,
valuables, heavy items

SOUTH (Mars)
Good placement for:
dining room, bedroom
(avoid putting main
entrance here)

SOUTHEAST (Venus)
Good placement for:
kitchen, fireplace,
computers, garage,
exercise, bath

Vastu considers the home to be a temple for our body, mind, and spirit. Here are some ways that you can create a sacred space in which to learn, grow, and relate to your family and friends.

Building

If you are starting from scratch and building your own house, there are a few things you can look for to help optimize the benefits of your property. The best days to start building your home are Monday, Wednesday, Thursday, and Friday. It is also recommended to begin construction when the moon is waxing (growing full) rather than waning. It is better for the front door to face to the north or the east, to bring wealth and longevity. Try to avoid having shadows (tall trees or buildings) from the setting sun fall on your house.

COLOR

Keeping in mind that everything is connected, vastu recommends that there be a flow from room to room, and from inside to outside. One way to achieve that is with color.

VATA

Balancing colors for Vatas are warm or calming. Yellows and golds are very pleasing in the Vata decor. So are white, violet, blue, and deep reds. Avoid bright red—it's far too stimulating.

PITTA

Because Pittas tend to be hot, they need a cooling environment to stay in balance. Stick with soft, pastel colors to soothe away tension. Blues and greens are particularly beneficial, as are pinks and roses.

KAPHA

Kapha needs the stimulation of bright, hot colors. Pick up the energy level with reds and oranges.

	VATA	PITTA	KAPHA
Recommended colors for home and fashion	warm pastels yellows greens	cool, soft colors blues purples, roses silver	bright, bold colors reds yellows, golds oranges

Nature

To be more in tune with nature and its intelligence, bring nature indoors wherever possible. Besides plants and trees, items that are made naturally are also recommended. For example, clay pots, cotton rugs, woven baskets, shells, and fresh flowers all help to remind us of our connection with nature. Desktop fountains help to bring in the element of water. Scented candles bring in the element of fire. Open some windows in the morning to let in fresh air.

Quiet Space

It's always nice to have an area set aside in your home for quiet and meditation. In India, these are called "Puja," or prayer, rooms. This is a place where you can just relax and find inner peace. Additionally, within each room of your home, it is good to have a small area set aside to remind you of your connection with the Divine. This can be a shelf filled with figurines or spiritual sayings, an altar, or a special painting. Use whatever it is that is meaningful for you.

Clutter

Clutter in your environment creates clutter in your mind. You can't think as clearly or function as efficiently as you can in an orderly environment. Vastu recommends that clutter be kept to a minimum. Closet doors and bathroom doors should remain closed at all times. Keep drawers and cupboards closed as well, to avoid a feeling of clutter. Keep hallways clear so you can move about freely.

Books

Books represent knowledge and are a wonderful addition to the home. Keep books neatly arranged, and honor their presence. When books are accessible and easy to find, they are more likely to be read.

Family

Photographs of family help to personalize your space. Displaying pictures that remind you of loved ones and happy memories will bring good energy to a room. Artwork that your children make for you is also good to have around.

Products

Rather than using chemicals, which contain toxins or unpleasant odors, vastu recommends that we use natural products to clean our environments and our bodies. Clothing made of natural fabrics is better for our skin than synthetic blends. Wonderful organic products for the bathroom, such as lotions, scrubs, and oils, are now readily available. You can find some up-to-date sources and links in the Coffey Shop on my Web site (www.coffeytalk.com).

	VATA	PITTA	KAPHA
Aromatherapy, balancing fragrances	vanilla orange lavender pine	rose jasmine sandalwood peppermint	cinnamon basil eucalyptus musk

Outdoors

Create a space where you can sit outdoors and enjoy nature. Get a comfortable chair where you can relax in the evening air after a long day at work. Hang a bird feeder outside your kitchen window. Plant flowers that attract butterflies and other wildlife. Start an herb garden that you can use when cooking. Put a pool, pond, or fountain in the northeast corner of your yard so you can reap the benefits of the element of water.

Above all, make your home comfortable. Fill it with things that you love and that are meaningful to you. This is a place where you should want to be, a place that reflects who you are.

16

Now & Forever:
Tips on Leading a Vedic Life

Love is the cure,
for your pain will keep giving birth to more pain
until your eyes constantly exhale love
as effortlessly as your body yields its scent.
—RUMI

Now you know the basics of Ayurveda and are ready to incorporate some of the principles into your life. Wonderful! So, where should you start? The best place to begin is right where you are. A lot of what Ayurveda teaches makes sense because we know it to be true already. For example, don't smoke; smoking dulls the senses and makes you sick. Avoid alcohol and caffeine. Eat fresh, healthy foods. Be a nice person. These practices are all part of taking care of our bodies, minds, and spirits. When we are feeling good, we can enjoy every aspect of our lives and our relationships at the highest level.

Ayurvedic Massage (Abhyanga)

Ayurvedic massage offers many benefits. If done in the morning, it helps you to start your day relaxed, which is essential to maintaining balance. When done at night, it promotes a restful night's sleep. It doesn't matter when you choose to do the massage, but you will receive the optimum benefits if you do it every day. Because the quality of Vata is dry and cold, a warm oil massage provides an ideal balance for Vata types, though all types will notice increased health and vitality, especially during Vata season. The massage soothes the nervous system and the endocrine system, since skin produces endocrine hormones. It rejuvenates the skin, promoting a youthful appearance. It also eliminates toxins and tones the muscles.

Sesame oil is generally recommended for Ayurvedic massage because it helps to balance all three of the doshas. But feel free to choose one of the oils that is specific to your dosha. Sesame is great for Vata. Coconut and sunflower both work well for Pitta. Corn and olive oils are beneficial for balancing Kapha. You may also add herbs or fragrances to the oils, to personalize them for your needs. The entire massage requires only about 2 ounces of oil per person each time. This is a self-massage, so it's usually done alone and in the standing position, but there's no reason why you can't perform the massage together with your partner, if you are so inclined.

Before you begin, warm the oil to skin temperature. The easiest way to do this is to keep a small plastic squeeze bottle filled with oil, so when you want a massage, all you need to do is set the bottle in a bowl or cup of very hot water and wait a few minutes for the oil to reach skin temperature.

While the oil warms, lay out a towel to protect the carpet or floor from any oil that may spill.

When you are ready, drizzle a small amount of oil onto your scalp and massage it in with the palms of your hands. Use a clockwise, circular motion. Then gently massage your face and ears. If you have oily skin, avoid those areas that are prone to breakouts. Massaging the ears is excellent for balancing Vata.

Drizzle some oil in your palms and massage your neck, then move to your shoulders. Use a circular motion on your joints—shoulders, elbows, knees—and long up-and-down strokes on your limbs.

Be gentle to your torso. Use large, clockwise motions to massage the chest and stomach area.

Reach around to massage your back as best you can without straining.

Then massage your legs, ankles, and knees. Using the palm of your hands, vigorously massage your feet.

It is best to leave the oil on the body for twenty minutes before washing it off in a warm (not hot) shower or bath. You can use this time to meditate or do your yoga exercises. If you don't have time to wait, that's fine. It's much better to do a quick massage than none at all.

MEDITATION

Ayurveda recognizes meditation as one of the most powerful tools for restoring balance in our mind and body. In this return to silence, we experience a deep sense of peace and relaxation. This reduces the stress that so often triggers the imbalance in our lives that in turn leads to health problems.

Deepak Chopra has revived "Primordial Sound Meditation," which originates from the ancient knowledge of India. In this technique, you use a personal mantra (sound), which is determined by your time and place of birth. When you silently repeat these Primordial Sounds, they still your mind and soothe your entire physiology—mind, body, and soul. Primordial Sound Meditation is easy to learn and does not require any specific belief or change in behavior or lifestyle. There are teachers and classes all over the world, and you can find one near you by visiting www.chopra.com.

There are many other types of meditation; whichever you choose, Ayurveda recommends that you practice twenty to thirty minutes in the morning and another twenty to thirty minutes in the evening. Time spent in silence or with nature helps keep the doshas in balance and can greatly improve your health and outlook on life. Ayurvedic researchers have found that meditation increases longevity and quality of life and can actually reverse the aging process.

Meditation Techniques

Here are some varieties you can try:

Witnessing

Witnessing is a pure form of meditation. It is simply sitting in meditation and watching the thoughts that come and go without judging or commenting. It is interesting to see what your moment-to-moment thoughts consist of from a completely neutral position. With this meditation, you're essentially stepping outside of yourself to observe. It gives you a different vantage point. You see that you are not your thoughts, but you are the thinker of your thoughts.

Watching the Breath

Watching the breath is sometimes called "mindfulness" meditation. It is a Buddhist meditation that focuses on the rise and fall of the breath. It's based on the idea that while the mind is engaged in focusing on your breathing it cannot focus on its usual distractions. In this meditation, your breathing should be gentle and regular. Just allow it to be the place where your mind is focused and enjoy the feeling of witnessing breathing rather than concentrating on it.

Sitting

This is the basic meditation of Zen Buddhists, for whom the path of enlightenment is everyday life lived with awareness and totality. Like all meditations, sitting is a tool to help us rediscover the immediacy and freshness of ordinary life, as we did as children. In this meditation, you just sit and allow whatever happens to happen. Your mind will try to distract you with past and present concerns, to take you away from fully experiencing the moment. Zen Buddhists believe these transient thoughts are "paper tigers" and that paying attention to them only gives them more energy. In the sitting meditation, you experience the fact that you are not the mind and can ignore its chatter at will. If your mind is particularly rebellious, you can distract it by concentrating on your breathing. Kaphas, who enjoy the peace and quiet, do very well with the sitting meditation.

Gazing

Another meditation device used to still the mind is gazing. The object that you look at is not really important. Traditional objects include a lighted candle, a flower, a religious image, or a picture of a guru. The main point of the exercise is to keep your eyes on a central spot because not moving the eyes restricts the amount of information for your brain to process. The idea is to keep your mind quiet by keeping your thoughts simple. When you start to think about something else, keep bringing your attention back to the object of your contemplation. The goal of your meditation is to feel the quality of the object, to relax, and to enjoy what you are seeing. Pittas, because they are so visual, respond well to gazing meditations.

Listening

Meditation is centered in the idea of relaxing and non-doing. When you are thinking, you may hear but you cannot truly listen. If you center your awareness in music, chanting, or natural sounds, you experience the essence of the sound, giving yourself the experience of emptiness, clarity, and receptivity. Vatas, who are sensitive to sounds, enjoy this kind of meditation.

Meditation in Action

Everything can become a meditation, including the most ordinary everyday chores. What transforms daily activities into meditation in action is awareness and wholeheartedness. The application of the Zen principle of giving undivided attention to, and really feeling the quality of, each of your actions is exemplified in the Japanese tea ceremony and the art of flower arranging. We can bring this same quality of attention to driving, standing in line at the store, or paying bills. Being present in the moment imparts an unmistakable peace, effortlessness, and enjoyment of the "little things" that make up the greater whole of life.

Silence

Today's lifestyle is hectic and crazy. We're constantly bombarded with noise in every way, shape, and form. The phone, the fax, the pager, the microwave, the computer, the TV, the car radio—everything seems to be fighting for our attention! We need some space, in the form of silence, to keep our sanity. Meditation offers that. It gives us some time to just "be."

When we meditate with other people, the effects are amplified. The vibratory level is raised so that each person participating receives more benefits. And those vibrations actually extend beyond ourselves out into our communities, so that by meditating, we're not only helping ourselves, we're helping the world. Meditating with a partner is a wonderful way to spend time together. It is communicating at a higher level, one beyond words. The famous Vedic teacher Swami Sivananda said in 1945, "Silence is the language of God."

Being completely silent with someone is an intimate experience. You can tell how close you feel to someone by how much time you spend together in silence. If you are aware of those "awkward pauses" and feel like you need to fill up the space with conversation, then you probably don't feel that you can let your guard down with that person.

Try spending one whole day, either by yourself, or with a loved one, in complete silence. This means no talking, but also no television, no radio, and no reading—reading is still mental activity because you're listening to the writer's words in your head. The idea is tune in to your inner wisdom—to be quiet for long enough to hear, and pay attention to, the intelligence of the universe.

There is so much to say about the topic of meditation that I have created a Web site (www.psmeditation.com) just for that purpose. I have posted articles and keep updated information about various meditation techniques to help enhance your practice. Come by and visit sometime.

DIGESTION

Your mind-body type will determine what kinds of foods you should favor and what kinds of exercise you should do. But regardless of mind-body type, there are certain things that everyone can do on a daily basis to benefit from Ayurveda. You can choose to do as much or as little as is comfortable for your lifestyle. The longer you practice Ayurveda, the easier it becomes, until it is second nature.

Food plays a big role in the Ayurvedic lifestyle routine. There are three parts to the digestive process that are important: digestion of food, assimilation of food, and elimination of food. When our digestion is efficient, the rest follows more easily, so we get the optimal benefit from our food and we are more in balance. There is a Vedic expression that says that if our digestion is strong, our bodies can turn poison into nectar, but if our digestion is weak, we can turn nectar into poison. The digestive fire is called *agni* in Sanskrit. Ayurveda offers the following guidelines to all of us who want to boost our agni and improve our digestion:

+ Sit down while you eat. Eat in a quiet atmosphere. Focus on the food; do not read or watch TV as you eat.
+ Don't rush through meals or linger over them too long.
+ Eat meals at approximately the same times every day.
+ Stop eating before you are completely full.
+ Allow approximately three to six hours between meals for digestion.
+ Eat when you are hungry, when the stomach is empty.
+ Sip warm water or juice with meals. Drink milk separately from meals, either alone or with other sweet foods.
+ Avoid ice-cold food and beverages.
+ Sit quietly for a few minutes after eating.

This chart shows specifically which tastes are best for each dosha.

	VATA	PITTA	KAPHA
Digestion tends to be	variable, delicate	strong, intense	slow, heavy
Appetite	variable	strong, hates missing meals or having late meals	constant

Diet	Tastes	Tastes	Tastes
To keep in balance, favor	sweet sour salty warm foods	sweet astringent bitter cool (not cold) foods	bitter pungent astringent warm, light foods

Here are some examples of specific foods in those taste categories that are balancing for each dosha:

SWEET	SOUR	SALTY	BITTER	PUNGENT	ASTRINGENT
sugar	lemon	salt	bitter greens	chili peppers	beans
honey	cheese		cucumber	onions	alfalfa sprouts
rice	yogurt		tonic water	garlic	apple
milk	tomato		spinach	ginger	pear
butter	grapes			cinnamon	potato
bread	plums				
	vinegar				

	VATA	PITTA	KAPHA
Fruits	Sweet, soft fruit is best: apricots, avocados, bananas, blueberries, cherries, grapes, mangoes, melons, papaya, peaches, pineapples.	Avoid fruits that are sour or unripe. Favor apples, avocados, cherries, coconuts, figs, mangoes, melon, sweet oranges, pears, raisins.	Avoid fruits that are sweet, sour, or very juicy. Choose apples, apricots, cranberries, pears, pomegranates; dried fruits are good.
Vegetables	Vegetables should be cooked, not raw. Favor asparagus, beets, carrots, green beans, sweet potatoes, onions.	Favor asparagus, broccoli, cabbage, cauliflower, green beans, leafy greens, lettuce, okra, peas, potatoes, sweet peppers, zucchini.	Almost all vegetables are good for Kapha, except for sweet and juicy vegetables such as: cucumbers, tomatos, sweet potatoes, zucchini.
Grains	Choose oats (cooked as cereal), rice, wheat.	Choose barley, oats, wheat, white rice.	Avoid hot cereals and steamed grains. Choose barley, buckwheat, corn, millet, rye.
Meats	Avoid red meat. Choose, in small quantities, chicken, seafood, turkey.	Avoid red meat and most seafood. Choose, in small quantities, chicken, turkey, shrimp.	Avoid red meat and most seafood. Choose, in small quantities, chicken, shrimp, turkey.
Nuts and Seeds	All nuts are okay; almonds are best.	Avoid most nuts and seeds, except coconut, pumpkin seeds, sunflower seeds.	Avoid most nuts and seeds, except sunflower seeds, pumpkin seeds.

EXERCISE

Exercise is, of course, the other half of the equation for taking care of our bodies. We need to get up and move—some of us more than others! The basic rule in Ayurveda is to exercise to 75 percent of your capacity. Don't work out until you are exhausted and depleted. Stop when you are still feeling good but can see that time coming. This way, you will build up your stamina and strength.

Vatas tend to get worn out; they have a low reserve of energy. The worst thing they can do is to overextend themselves physically. Vatas are fairly flexible, so they love exercises like yoga or Pilates, where they can stretch and warm their muscles. They also like exercises where they can have fun, because they tend to get bored easily; anything new and interesting gets their attention. They love a hot, steamy shower after exercise.

Pittas are fiercely competitive, so sports where they play on a team, or games where they have something at stake, really fuel their fire. Swimming, diving, and other water sports are great for Pittas, because the water is cooling, which is balancing for them. It is refreshing for Pittas to take a nice dip in the pool after their workouts.

Kaphas have a lot of stored-up energy, so they can take more strenuous exercise—actually, they need to burn off that energy so that it doesn't turn to bulk. Running is great, even if it's on a treadmill at the gym. Weight lifting is also really good for Kaphas. As a reward for their efforts, Kaphas may look forward to a nice warm soak in the tub!

	VATA	PITTA	KAPHA
Recommended exercise for balance	**Activities** Low-impact: yoga walking dancing	**Activities** Competitive or team sports: baseball tennis or cooling sports: swimming	**Activities** stimulating, regular exercise: bodybuilding running

BEHAVIOR

Just as we feed our bodies healthy food, it is imperative to feed our minds with material that is good for us as well. Ayurveda recommends reading the Bhagavad Gita for spiritual nourishment. From this text, a set of *rasayanas,* or behavioral recommendations, has been developed. It is said that following these instructions will help you avoid contradictions in the mind and therefore prevent physiological strain.

BEHAVIOR RASAYANAS

+ Be honest and kind
+ Be free from anger
+ Abstain from immoderate behavior
+ Be nonviolent and calm
+ Observe cleanliness in yourself and your environment
+ Be charitable toward others
+ Observe a regular daily routine
+ Be loving and compassionate
+ Be respectful, especially to teachers and elders
+ Keep the company of the wise
+ Be modest, have good manners
+ Follow your religious beliefs, be self-disciplined
+ Keep a positive outlook
+ Devote yourself to the development of higher states of consciousness

It is not necessary to memorize these rasayanas, as doing so may put strain on the mind. But reading them every day will remind you of the simple things you can do to help yourself and, in turn, to help the world.

ROUTINE

It is easy to incorporate a few Ayurvedic principles into your lifestyle. Here is an example of a daily routine that anyone can follow. Of course, it can be personalized to fit your particular schedule, so don't feel that you must adhere to every little bit of it. For example, if you need to drive the kids to school in the morning, it is probably better to meditate after they are out of the house! Remember, whenever you can meditate with your partner, the vibrations are amplified, and the experience is much richer. Coordinate your meditation times whenever possible and you will see that it will help to strengthen your relationship.

IDEAL DAILY AYURVEDIC ROUTINE

- Wake up at sunrise, about 6:00 AM
- Use the bathroom
- Brush your teeth and tongue
- Give yourself an Ayurvedic massage
- Do your yoga stretches and/or your exercise program
- Take a warm shower or bath
- Meditate
- Eat a light breakfast based on your mind-body type diet
- Work or study
- Eat lunch, your largest meal of the day, at the same time each day, between noon and 1:00 PM
- Work or study
- Meditate before dinner
- Eat a light dinner, at the same time each day, preferably before 6:30 PM
- Take a short walk, to aid digestion
- Relax; read; listen to music; visit with friends
- Get to bed by 10:00 PM

If your mornings are hectic and you need to leave the house very early, you may choose to do your massage and shower in the evening. Doing so will give you an especially restful night's sleep. If you wake up hungry, as many of us do, you may choose to eat breakfast before your shower. Ayurveda will prove beneficial in whatever way it is blended into your routine. Even adding just a couple of new things into your established routine will give you a good start.

It is nice to take your time in the morning and fit in all of the Ayurvedic routine, but if you are in a hurry, it is better to do some or all of it quickly, rather than to skip it altogether.

BALANCE

Keeping your mind and body in balance is an ongoing commitment that will keep you healthy. The Ayurvedic lifestyle may seem different at first, just because it's not what you're used to, but once you get into the routine and experience the benefits of increased energy and vitality, you'll love it!

17

PRANA & PLANETS:
USING THE ENERGY IN AND AROUND YOU
TO ENHANCE YOUR RELATIONSHIPS

These just
aren't words you are reading.
If you churn them, you could have some
good cream.
—RUMI

WHEN YOU ARE feeling good, healthy, and in balance, you are better able to contribute to healthy and balanced relationships in your life. By now you probably have a pretty good understanding of how the doshas are expressed in you, and in nature, and how everything is connected. This chapter explores how we are all connected on many different levels. You'll discover how you can tap into the energy that is within you and all around you to grow and enhance your relationships.

In the Tantra section of Chapter 12, we talked a little bit about touch as one of the five senses. There are many reasons why touch is so important in a relationship. Touch is a form of communication. It can be healing, and it can be a turn-on.

THE SUBTLE BODY

Both tantra and Ayurveda explain that when we get close enough to a person to touch them, we have achieved a certain amount of intimacy. We are "in their space," so to speak. We each have our physical body, and a subtle body. All around our physical body is a kind of light that is a part of our subtle body. This light, called our *aura,* isn't always visible to the eye, but we can train ourselves to feel it with our hands. It's almost like when you can feel the heat rising off a person's skin. Our auras radiate from us.

We also have several energy centers in our bodies. There are seven main energy centers, five of which are located roughly along the inside of the spine. These energy centers are called *chakras,* which means "wheel" in Sanskrit. If we were to draw a picture of a chakra, it would look like a wheel with flower petals around it— which is how the name came about. While the chakras reside in our physical body, they are actually part of our subtle, non-physical body, just as the aura is.

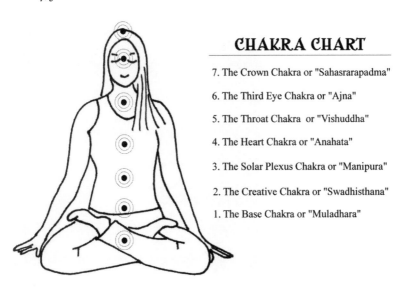

CHAKRA CHART

7. The Crown Chakra or "Sahasrarapadma"

6. The Third Eye Chakra or "Ajna"

5. The Throat Chakra or "Vishuddha"

4. The Heart Chakra or "Anahata"

3. The Solar Plexus Chakra or "Manipura"

2. The Creative Chakra or "Swadhisthana"

1. The Base Chakra or "Muladhara"

This chart indicates the approximate positioning of the seven major chakras.

PRANA

Prana in Sanskrit means "breath." In Vedic texts, prana is recognized as the energy of spiritual light, and this is the substance of our subtle body. Prana is an energy that can be transferred from one person to another, through various hands-on treatments such as massage. We energize our prana through meditation, yoga, mantra practice, and by eating nutritious foods. Another way to work on our prana is through *pranayama,* or yogic breathing exercises.

We all need to breathe to survive. Even plants breathe. Although breathing appears to be a kind of mechanical process, one we don't really think about, Ayurveda explains that the process of inhaling and exhaling is full of life itself. Notice how the breath changes when our emotions come into play. When we are scared, we tense up and hold our breath, and our breathing is irregular. When we are happy and laughing, we breathe deeply and our breathing is rhythmic. *Pranayama* means "to control the breath." By doing so, we are helping to settle and control our busy minds.

Pranayama is often considered an art, and some people consider it an important part of their spiritual practice. Our bodies are made up of pairs of things: two arms, two legs, two lungs, two nostrils, and even two brains, left and right. Pranayama helps us even out the balance of energy on both sides, including our Shiva and Shakti, male and female energy. This brings us a greater sense of awareness.

There are many different types of pranayama, but let's look at just three:

1. Alternate Nostril Breathing Pranayama

This exercise is good for all three doshas.

✦ Begin by sitting with your back straight. Be comfortable, either on the floor or in a chair.
✦ Take your right-hand thumb, and with it, close your right nostril.
✦ Inhale through your left nostril, deep into the diaphragm. Hold it for a moment.

✦ Close your left nostril with the ring finger of your right hand.
✦ Exhale through your right nostril. Hold it a moment.
✦ Inhale through your right nostril. Hold it a moment.
✦ Close your right nostril with your right thumb and begin the sequence again.

Do this exercise for eight to ten "rounds" and you will notice an increase in your energy level and feel like you have a clearer mind.

2. Cooling Pranayama
This exercise is particularly good for Pittas.

✦ Curl your tongue into a tube shape and stick it out a little. If you can't curl your tongue, then part your lips, keeping your teeth together, and put your tongue up against your teeth.
✦ Inhale through your mouth, allowing the air to pass over your tongue.
✦ Draw your tongue in and close your mouth.
✦ Swallow.
✦ Exhale through the nose, keeping the mouth closed.

3. Breath of Fire Pranayama
This exercise is good for both Vatas and Kaphas.

✦ Inhale gently through the nose.
✦ Exhale through the nose more actively, with more strength, almost like you're blowing something out of your nose.
✦ Inhale gently again.
✦ Blow out through the nose again.
✦ Start out slowly, then gradually increase your speed. The idea is to sound like a train moving slowly at first, and then picking up speed. Practice one round of twenty to thirty exhales, then rest for a minute or so. You can practice up to five rounds at a time, twice a day.

The Chakras

The chakras work with the five elements (earth, water, fire, air, and ether) to provide energy to various parts of the mind and body. When our chakras are functioning well, we are healthier and happier. One way to enliven the chakras is by touching the physical body.

CHAKRA (SANSKRIT NAME)	ASSOCIATED COLOR	LOCATION	ELEMENT	INFLUENCES	SENSE	DOSHA
Muladhara	red	base of the spine	earth	energy of elimination	smell	Kapha
Swadhisthana	orange	between the navel and the base of the spine	water	fertility, sexual energy, creativity	taste	Kapha
Manipura	yellow	the navel area, the solar plexus	fire	the stomach, the energy of digestion, absorption	sight	Pitta
Anahata	green	the heart	air	the heart, the energy for circulation and respiration, supports the immune system	touch	Vata
Vishuddha	blue	the throat	ether	speech, thyroid	sound	Vata
Ajna	indigo	between and slightly above the brows (third eye)	mind (combination of all)	the brain	intuition	All three doshas

The seventh chakra (*sahasrara*) is often called the crown chakra. It located at the top of the head, and its color is violet. You can see that the colors of the chakras correspond with the colors of the rainbow. And, like those colors, you can remember the sequence with the name ROY G. BIV, for the first letters in red, orange, yellow, green, blue, indigo, and violet.

We have other, smaller chakras in the palms of our hands and the soles of our feet. So, by touching others, we meld our energy with theirs. The best way to hug someone, to make that person really feel good and hugged, is to embrace him or her heart to heart. Put your left palm on the base of the person's spine, and with your right hand open, rub up and down his or her back.

MASSAGE

With massage we are working our hands on the body, manipulating muscles and skin. And we are also working with these energies; there is an interaction between giver and receiver.

When giving a massage, you need to be aware of this, so you can focus on giving loving, caring energy to your partner. Be careful to keep the person's dosha in mind, as well as his or her preferences in relation to pressure and temperature. Think good thoughts, and keep your vibrational level high. Massage is a service, and it should be offered to your partner as a heartfelt gift. Breathe deeply. After the massage, it is a good idea to restore your energy by relaxing yourself a little bit.

The receiver needs to just relax and give in to the experience. Allow the body to surrender and not resist. Close your eyes, find a place of peace, and enjoy.

Some general rules to keep in mind when giving a massage:

✦ Warm your hands by rubbing them together.
✦ Use an oil to lubricate your hands to avoid friction or irritation.
✦ Be gentle on the parts of the body that are more thin.
✦ The feet may be massaged more vigorously, and for a longer time.
✦ If there is hair on any part of the body, massage in the direction of hair growth.
✦ Use plant-based oils only. Mineral oils do not get absorbed by the skin and can actually be irritating, because they prevent the skin from breathing.

Massage balances all three doshas and is particularly healing for
Vatas. There are many different oils you can use, depending on the
season and the dosha of the person you are working on. For Vatas,
warm the oil to body temperature, be generous with your portions, and use gentle, firm strokes. For Pittas, the oil should be
slightly cool; use a moderate amount, and keep your touch light
and soothing. For Kaphas, you may use a dry massage, or use just a
small amount of warm oil. Kaphas can take a stronger touch, a
deeper massage.

	VATA	PITTA	KAPHA
Balancing massage oil	sesame, almond, castor	coconut, sunflower	olive, corn, mustard

Yoga for Two

Yoga is one exercise that is beneficial and balancing for all of the
doshas. It is also an exercise that you can do with your partner, to
touch and get to know each other better. Yoga postures are called
asanas; there are many asanas that you can do individually or as a
couple. Most yoga studios are now offering "date nights," when
couples can practice together. You may also choose to just try practicing at home.

	VATA	PITTA	KAPHA
Focus of practice	calming, grounding	cooling, relaxing	energizing, releasing
Recommended asanas	Sun Salutation Lotus, Lion, Tree, Triangle, Warrior, Inversions, Cobra, Tortoise, Boat, Twist, Corpse	Moon Salutation, Triangle, Half Moon, Shoulder Stand, Boat, Fish, Bow, Tortoise.	Sun Salutation, Lion, Half Moon, Downward Dog, Upward Dog, Handstand, Headstand, Shoulder Stand, Plow, Camel

Practicing yoga with a partner helps you get "in touch" with that person and also with yourself. Yoga helps us to look within, to challenge ourselves, to be still. When working with another person, that person acts as a kind of mirror for us and helps to keep us on track. There is also a certain amount of trust involved when you are doing asanas together. There are times when you need to depend on your partner for support or balance, and this can reflect how you function within the relationship in other ways, too. A lot of feelings can come up, so this is a good opportunity for growth, both individually and as a couple.

Another benefit of yoga is simply the physical exercise—yoga helps us to keep fit. When we are in good shape, we feel better, and we are able to perform better, mentally and physically. Yoga is also a way to relax and just have fun together. It is a shared activity that allows us to escape our hectic schedules and spend time on a joint project with our partners, where we can set and accomplish goals together. So yoga is a bonding experience in many ways. Practicing yoga together can help both you and your partner to reduce stress, improve your communication, develop trust and understanding, and enhance your libido.

Here are some basic tips:

✦ Find a flat, open space where you are free to move around without bumping into anything.

✦ Set aside at least thirty minutes, and preferably an hour, to devote to this practice and nothing else. Turn off the phones.

✦ Don't practice on a full stomach. Allow time to digest before exercising. If you are pregnant or have back problems, consult your doctor before starting any new exercise program.

✦ Wear loose, comfortable clothing and bare feet.

✦ Don't overdo it. Rest when you feel tired. Your stamina will increase with regular practice.

✦ Breathe through your nose. Your breaths should be long and deep. Breathe with your diaphragm. Relax your chest and allow your breath to feel as if it is coming from your belly.

✦ Start out slowly; allow your body to warm up.

✦ Have fun. Laugh. Enjoy being together. Don't take yourself too seriously.

✦ Cool down gently, allow your body time to rest and restore itself after you are done.

Some asanas can be done facing each other; other poses can be done back to back. The idea is to take the asana and do it as a team. Integrate your practice with your partner's. For example, one of you can do a shoulder stand propped up against your partner's back instead of the wall. The seated partner can lend support by lifting the arms to steady the lifted legs behind him. Or you may try Half Moon Pose, with one person helping the other to balance by lifting and raising the extended leg. It's really like dancing. You get to know each other's moves, and how you fit together. You develop a kind of rhythm and get comfortable with each other after a while. This brings an intimacy, a closeness that is both physical and emotional, that really strengthens a relationship.

JYOTISH

Just as love is a dance between two people, life is a dance between us and the universe. We are all one, so what affects the universe affects each one of us in some way. And it works both ways! The Vedic sages have studied this dance and come up with a system for working with cosmic energy to help guide us along the way.

Vedic astrology is called *Jyotish*. In Sanskrit, *jyot* means "light," and *ish* comes from the word *ishwara,* which means nature. Jyotish is known as "the study of light." The light is the light from the stars and the planets, and also the light of consciousness. Like Ayurveda, Jyotish gives us tools for learning about other people and ourselves and how we relate. Used with Ayurveda, Jyotish adds an interesting dimension to the way we look at relationships.

CHARTS

A Jyotish practitioner is called a *Jyotishi*. A Jyotishi will make up your astrological chart and determine which planets fall in which houses. The difference between the Western system of astrology and Jyotish is that the Western system looks at the relationship of the sun to the Earth and the seasons. The Vedic system looks at the Sun's position in relation to the stars. Western astrology is referred to as "tropical" and Vedic astrology is called "sidereal."

Over the years, the two systems have drifted apart a bit; there now is a 24-degree difference between where each system considers the start of the astrological year to be. This causes the whole wheel to shift, so in Jyotish, your Western sun sign may be moved back by one whole sign. For example, my birthday is April 25. In Western astrology, my sun sign is Taurus, but in Jyotish, my sun sign is in Aries. In Western astrology, the chart is drawn as a wheel, but in Jyotish, it is drawn as a square, or a box of triangles.

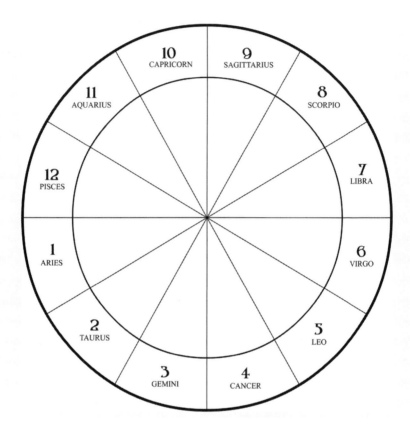

WESTERN ASTROLOGICAL CHART

This is the chart that is traditionally used in Western astrology. Starting with Aries in the equinox position, the chart is read counter-clockwise.

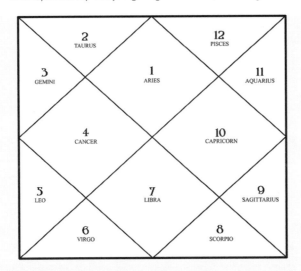

12 PISCES	1 ARIES	2 TAURUS	3 GEMINI
11 AQUARIUS			4 CANCER
10 CAPRICORN			5 LEO
9 SAGITTARIUS	8 SCORPIO	7 LIBRA	6 VIRGO

NORTH INDIAN JYOTISH CHART

The North Indian Jyotish chart is read from right to left.
Some Jyotishis say that just gazing at this chart can bring benefits.

SOUTH INDIAN JYOTISH CHART

The South Indian Jyotish chart is read from left to right.
This chart style is used in areas such as Bombay and Bangalore.

Jyotish and Ayurveda are complementary sciences and are often practiced in tandem in India. Ayurvedic doctors (called *Vaidyas*) may consult a patient's astrological chart for diagnostic purposes. The chart helps to explain some of our personality traits, as well. For example, Vatas are notoriously bad at saving money. But if a Vata person has Jupiter, a Kapha planet, in the astrological house that deals with money, this may cause the person to adopt more Kapha-like skills in that area and be cautious with money. As you can see, we can get much more detailed information when we combine the practice of Ayurveda with Jyotish.

By looking at the charts of two partners, we can see where karma comes into play. Karma is action, and the effects of our actions. When two people help each other out and bring out the best in each other, this creates beneficial karma for both of them, and the relationship is a positive one. If they bring each other down and tend toward unhealthy habits, then they activate bad karma, and the relationship is negative. A Jyotishi can analyze the two charts to determine in what areas a couple will get along, and in what areas they will have challenges. In India, Jyotishis are consulted before a marriage takes place, so the couple is fully aware of what they are getting into.

RASA

Jyotish also helps to explain why we are attracted to certain people. *Rasa,* or taste, is not just in the mouth, but also in the mind. When we're drawn to a certain type of individual we say that we have that "taste" in people. Rasa also means juice, and emotion, in every sense of that word. So we could say that when we desire someone, we crave that person's juice. As our emotions get involved, we want to taste that person, kiss him or her. Jyotish helps us get past the base desires, to look beyond the emotions to the practicality of dealing with mundane everyday issues that can make or break a relationship.

ASTRAL BODY	SANSKRIT NAME	GOVERNED TASTE	DOSHA
Sun	Surya	bitter	Pitta
Moon	Chandra	salty	Kapha and Vata
Mars	Mangala	pungent	Pitta
Mercury	Budha	various flavors	Can be any of the three, or a mix of all
Jupiter	Guru	sweet	Kapha
Venus	Sukra	sour	Kapha and Vata
Saturn	Shani	astringent	Vata
North node of the Moon	Rahu	-	Vata
South node of the Moon	Ketu	-	Pitta

TIMING

Timing is another way that Jyotish can help with our relationships. With gardening, we want to plant seeds at the appropriate times to ensure the best outcome for our crops. And with our relationships, we can choose astrologically auspicious times to begin our endeavors to encourage their best outcome. There are so many details and specifics to consider when comparing two Jyotish charts, it is best to consult a Jyotishi for your own personal situations. But here are some general rules, just to give you an idea of the kinds of things that Jyotish addresses.

The best days for a wedding are, in this order: Thursday, Friday, Monday, Wednesday and Sunday. Thursday is best because it is ruled by Jupiter, the largest planet, (generally considered the luckiest planet.) Friday is good because it is ruled by Venus, which is often called the planet of love. The moon represents domesticity and nurture, so a Monday wedding emphasizes those qualities in a marriage. Wednesday is ruled by Mercury, which brings good communication. Sunday is fairly neutral, because the Sun represents independence.

Tuesdays and Saturdays are generally not recommended for weddings. Mars governs Tuesday and is associated with turbulence. It is also a Pitta planet, and one of the negative emotions of Pitta is anger. Because Saturn is so distant, it has isolated, cold, dim connotations, so therefore Saturday is often avoided as a wedding day in India.

However, all this should be taken with a grain of salt. In the West, we have other considerations to deal with, such as when the facility is available and when the relatives are able to travel! Remember, with an Ayurvedic lifestyle we're not supposed to stress ourselves out. A Jyotishi who understands the Western mind-set will be able to take this into account and make a recommendation by looking at the whole picture.

There are other things that a Jyotishi will look at when determining a wedding day for a couple. One is, Venus should be visible. When Venus, the planet of love and celebration, is visible, it is like a blessing on the marriage. It is also preferred to schedule the wedding during daylight hours. Light is associated with awareness, and it is important that the couple be seeing clearly, or going into the marriage with their eyes open. For the same reason, it is also beneficial to choose a date with a bright moon. Ideally, it is best for a wedding to take place during a full moon, or close to that date. It is better to marry when the moon is waxing (meaning approximately the two-week period when the moon is "growing" from new to full) rather than waning. And it is preferable not to schedule the ceremony around the few days before and after the new moon, when there is little light in the sky.

My husband and I consulted a Jyotishi before our wedding. We had our charts done and had a compatibility analysis. The information we got was really valuable for us. It kind of fine-tuned what we had already learned about each other from our doshas. Our Jyotishi also helped us select a wedding date. We wanted to get married outside, so the weather was a consideration. We ended up choosing August 4, which worked out on many levels. Even though it was a Saturday, the other factors far outweighed the day-of-the-week issue. First of all, the place was available and our friends could all attend! That was important to us, of course. Also, there was a full moon, which was great. The Jyotishi pointed out that the number 4 is significant in both of our charts, so the August 4 date would bring us extra luck. We scheduled the wedding for 4:30 in the afternoon, just for an added bonus. It was a beautiful day, and a happy one, too!

Jyotish can be used for the timing of any important event—starting a business, building a home, or changing jobs. You can get a compatibility chart analysis for business partners or for parents and children, to help find out where your challenges are and figure out how to better deal with them.

Jyotish tells us that we can either placate or modify the influence of a particular planet by wearing its corresponding gemstone. A Jyotishi will "prescribe" a certain stone, the size, shape, the metal it is set in, and even how to wear it, based on your individual chart. Certain stones, determined to be "Jyotish quality," are used for this purpose. Usually size matters, and stones of one carat or larger are said to be more powerful. But there are ways around this; you may wear a semi-precious stone of the same color, if you don't want to spend the big bucks. Again, don't strain in any way!

Choosing your stone is a personal decision; it needs to "feel" right, and it has to be pleasing to you. It is also best for the stone to be set so that it touches your skin, for the maximum benefits. Then when you have the stone cut in the proper shape, set in the recommended metal, in a pendant or a ring, and know where it is to be worn, you begin wearing your new piece of jewelry on the appropriate day.

ASTRAL BODY	COLOR	GEMSTONE	WEEKDAY
Sun	deep red, orange	ruby	Sunday
Moon	bright white	pearl	Monday
Mars	medium-red	red coral	Tuesday
Mercury	green	emerald	Wednesday
Jupiter	gold, yellow	yellow sapphire	Thursday
Venus	medium-white	diamond	Friday
Saturn	blue, black	blue sapphire	Saturday
Rahu (north node of the moon)	brown	garnet	Saturday
Ketu (south node of the moon)	multicolor	cat's-eye	Tuesday

There are certain gemstones recommended to help balance out the doshas, too. This is helpful to know when shopping for your sweetie!

	VATA	PITTA	KAPHA
Beneficial	ruby or garnet	pearl	ruby or garnet
gemstones	yellow sapphire or topaz	lapis lazuli	cat's-eye
	emerald or aquamarine	emerald or aquamarine	blue sapphire
	onyx	diamonds	
		red coral	
		opal	
Beneficial metals	gold	silver	copper

18

Appetites & Aphrodisiacs:
How to Live Your Life "In Love"

The nut tastes sweet; I bet the prayer
spiced it up somehow.
—RUMI

THE AYURVEDIC LIFESTYLE is all about keeping us healthy and in balance in body, mind, and spirit. It's also about keeping our relationships thriving. Love nourishes us. Love is our true nature. When we are in love we feel happy, and our bodies give off a neuro-psycho immune response. Studies have shown that love causes us to literally produce healing chemicals for ourselves!

We can choose to live our lives "in love," and this chapter shows you a few ways to do just that.

LOVE

As human beings, we are drawn to love. However, in the West, there is often a bravado of independence. And in reality, we truly are whole and complete on our own. "Alone" comes from the words "all in one." The problem is that when we are alone we are often lonely, and loneliness is a state of psychological dis-ease. This is a big issue in our culture. We tend to put up a fence around ourselves, thinking that we are being protective. But living behind a fence, or being "defensive" causes more loneliness. Feelings of isolation lead us to feel separate from all of creation. This doesn't need to be the case.

Love is sweet, and love is soft. When we love someone we have nicknames for that person, often it's "Honey," "Sweetie," or "Sugarpie." It sounds silly, but it makes us smile, and it conveys how we feel. Love is divine. It gives us clarity and helps us see things in a more beautiful light. With love come compassion, understanding, acceptance, and sharing. Expressing love makes us better people.

In Vedanta, there are four yogas, or paths, through which to pursue our spirituality. The word *yoga* comes from the root Sanskrit word *yuj,* which means "to yoke," or "to unite." The practice of yoga helps us to unite with our spirits.

Jnana yoga is the path of knowledge. This is the path that is directed by the mind. To follow this path, we use affirmations to remind ourselves about what is real, and what is the truth. This "right thinking" helps us to shed the veil of illusion and see ourselves as we truly are, pure, perfect, and free. Jnana yoga takes reasoning, and Pittas, who are so good at intellectualizing, may be drawn to this path.

Karma yoga is the path of work. But it is work without attachment to the end result. Rather than working for a paycheck, it is working as a spiritual offering. You could also call this the path of service. The path of Karma yoga explains that working for money, promotions, or praise leads us to disappointment, because we can never meet all of our expectations—it is never "enough." Instead, when we work or perform actions as a service to ourselves and to others, we can experience spirit in everything we do. Vatas, who are so active and not usually motivated by money, may be drawn to Karma yoga.

Raja yoga is known as the path of meditation. The idea is that by stilling the mind through meditation, we can experience more of our true selves. It explains that we need to settle the mind, which is constantly stirred up with thoughts just as a lake is muddied through activity. When the lake settles down, the water becomes clear; so it goes with our mind. This tranquil state of mind lets us think clearly and see what is important in life. Kaphas, who like to be still and quiet, may be attracted to Raja yoga.

Bhakti yoga is the path of love. *Bhakti* means devotion. It is said that through love and devotion, we discover who we truly are. This is love of all creation. When we love without expectation, we experience the greatest feeling there is. Love is pure awareness.

There is a power, a positive energy, that comes with love, and we can utilize it for our spiritual growth. Vedanta explains that our love for others is unselfish and without motive when we can see the spirit within them. It is this spirit whom we truly love. So we can learn to look beyond the fabulous face and cute figure, all limiting qualities of the human rather than the divine, and instead experience love heart to heart. Love is available to all of us, and it is an irresistible force!

Part of the beauty of Ayurveda is that it teaches us to love people for who they are, to appreciate them for the qualities that are a part of their nature. So often we want to try to change people, to "mold" them to fit into our picture of how we think they "should" be with us. But Ayurveda shows us that this is not only pointless, it can be detrimental to a relationship. Instead, what we can do is to change our own perception, our own way of looking at things. This can be as simple as coming up with new, more positive ways of redefining for ourselves the traits and habits of the people we love. By doing this, we cast our partner in a much more flattering light, and show that we understand the value and the weight of our words. This is an important part of nurturing our relationships. Here are some examples:

INSTEAD OF SAYING YOUR VATA PARTNER IS	SAY THAT YOUR VATA PARTNER IS
hyper	energetic
nervous	cautious
weird	creative
abrupt	spontaneous
wishy-washy	flexible

INSTEAD OF SAYING YOUR PITTA PARTNER IS	SAY THAT YOUR PITTA PARTNER IS
nitpicky	discerning
a workaholic	ambitious
relentless	passionate
blunt	honest
a risk-taker	courageous

INSTEAD OF SAYING YOUR KAPHA PARTNER IS	SAY THAT YOUR KAPHA PARTNER IS
apathetic	mellow
lazy	relaxed
clingy	affectionate
predictable	dependable
a workhorse	high stamina

SEX

Without sex, there would be no life. And as long as there is life, there will be sex. Sex is creative energy, and it is profound.

Sex can be a spiritual experience. Vedanta explains that sexual desire is basically a longing for union with spirit, a higher love. Yet sex must be practiced responsibly if we are to benefit from it.

Yes, sex is natural, and a healthy sexual appetite is good. But sex is not good for us if we carry with it feelings of unworthiness or guilt. Like everything else in life, there needs to be a balance. By overindulging or suppressing our urges, we create problems for ourselves. Sex is best when it is an expression of love, when we can relax and truly be ourselves with the one we love.

Marriage is sacred, and it can also be a path to spiritual fulfillment. A person's life partner is a person's spiritual partner and must be regarded as such in every sense of the word. This means truthfulness, fidelity, and recognizing the divine within each other. When you have that level of trust and commitment, you can experience unity with each other, because you understand that you are truly uniting in spirit. You understand the "we" in terms of unity and oneness, and can set aside the "you" and "I" that is separateness. This brings you *moksha,* or ecstasy. It leads you back to knowing who you really are.

Marriage makes most of us feel liberated, as if we have found our soulmates and can clearly see beauty in all things. But how can you keep this feeling? It is a challenge in our Western world to maintain a deep, loving relationship when we have all kinds of outside distractions to contend with. The secret is to get beyond the trivial, beyond the ego, and to approach life as a journey that you are on together.

When you understand the principles of Ayurveda, you can see that many of your differences are there to serve you. They help to balance you out and to grow spiritually. There is no need for conflict, because you love and accept one another as you are, and you know that it works both ways. Your desires and passions become tools for self-knowledge in the context of a committed relationship.

Ayurveda explains that the role of sex is to bring creative energy into our relationships. It offers a few basic suggestions about how to enhance our sexual experiences.

- ✦ The best time to make love is between 7:00 PM and midnight, ideally between 10:00 PM and 11:00 PM
- ✦ A gentle massage after lovemaking helps to restore strength.
- ✦ Avoid sexual activity after a heavy meal, if you are hungry, or if you are angry.

The *Kama Sutra* was written over two thousand years ago by the Vedic sage Vatsyayana. *Kama Sutra* means "the science of love." This text, which is considered to be one of the most important manuals on love, proclaims that sexual equality and happiness can be enjoyed by every human being, and that sex can bring beauty and joy to a relationship. It says, "If men and women act according to each other's liking, their love for each other will not be lessened even in one hundred years." So, if you know what your lover likes and are sensitive to your lover's sexual style, your relationship will be that much more beautiful.

	VATA	PITTA	KAPHA
Sexual style	creative	passionate	loving
Libido	variable	moderate	low, constant
Commitment style	impulsive	deliberate	hesitant
Endurance	low	moderate	strong, steady

LIVING WELL

Food plays a big part in relationships—we spend a lot of time eating together, and this is valuable bonding time. Our rasas (tastes, juices, emotions), are intermingled. When you can mesh your eating habits, you will find the experience more satisfying. A vegetarian will have a hard time dining with a meat-eater if the sight of rare meat is a turn-off for him or her. These are important considerations when determining compatibility. A couple who eats meals together has a better chance of staying together than a couple whose diets are mutually disagreeable.

We all know how important it is to eat well to stay healthy, and we may even know the right foods to eat to keep us in balance. But in this hectic, crazy, fast-paced world it can still be difficult to maintain a good diet.

Part of the problem is that we're running around so much that we rely on "fast foods." Even when we're eating at home, making dinner can mean we take something out of a cardboard box in the freezer and zap it in the microwave. It doesn't have to be this way!

We just need to learn a few new habits to discover a way of eating that will nourish our bodies and souls.

Chapter 16 discusses Ayurveda's recommendations for each dosha in terms of tastes and specific foods. Now we're going to look at how you can use this information to come up with satisfying meals for yourself and your loved ones. You don't need to prepare different dishes for different people in the household. Ideally, an Ayurvedic meal consists of all the tastes—and in that way, your taste buds and your tummies will be pleased.

FOOD PREPARATION

The preparation of food is important in Ayurveda. Meals should be cooked with love and sweet intention. Whatever emotion you put into your cooking will be mixed into the food you are making. In the movie *Like Water for Chocolate* there is a scene where a girl is making stew. She is heartbroken that her beloved is to marry someone else, and her tears fall into the pot as she adds the vegetables and spices. When her family members eat the stew, they are overcome with grief and begin to cry. This is a powerful illustration of how emotion can affect the things we create.

It has often been said that chicken soup is the best remedy when someone is sick. And yet, probably the most potent medicinal ingredient is the love with which the soup is made. In that love is the real cure! So, don't cook when you are angry or sad. Cook with reverence, gratitude, appreciation, and love, and all those good things will be a part of what we take in during our meals.

Cooking can be therapeutic! It is a time for you to be creative and intuitive. The process of cooking itself can be a meditation, opening you up for inspiration. And cooking can be fun, too. It is a great way for you to spend time away from computers and phones, to relax and go with the flow.

PRESENTATION

Meal presentation is important, as well. Rather than eating in the driver's seat of your car, or standing up next to a counter, set a nice table for you and your loved ones. Clear the table of the mail and newspapers and use place mats or a nice tablecloth. Use "real" dishes rather than paper plates, and "real" utensils rather than plastic ones. Cloth napkins are a nice touch and are environmentally friendly, too. Candlelight adds a warm glow; be sure to use unscented candles so that the smell of the food is not overpowered. Pay attention to the colors in the room and on the plates; everything should go well together and be pleasing to the eye.

Before eating, take a few moments to express gratitude for the meal, for the people who prepared the meal, and for the time that is spent with loved ones. During the meal, show respect and appreciation for those at the table by observing etiquette and by encouraging everyone to participate in the conversation.

BALANCE

The biggest obstacle most of us face when trying to figure out just what to cook is time. There just never seems to be enough of it! And it's not just the cooking time, but the figuring-out-what-to-make time, the shopping-for-ingredients time, the eating time, and the clean-up time. If we followed all the great rules for the healthiest eating, we'd be living our lives around our meals, without any time for anything else! That's not good. Remember that Ayurveda is all about balance. The Ayurvedic lifestyle is meant to make our lives easier, so don't strain yourself. Above all else, it is important for us to be flexible.

Vegetarian Diet

For many reasons, a vegetarian diet is optimal. Studies have shown that people who don't eat animals have less risk of heart disease and cancer, the two biggest killers in our society today. In terms of ecology, it takes roughly sixteen pounds of grain fed to livestock to produce one pound of hamburger meat. So, eating meat causes a great burden on our global food resources. And then there is the issue of the emotions that permeate our food. There is fear and suffering for the animal that gives its life to become someone's dinner—do we really want to take that in?

The problem with a vegetarian diet is that most restaurants have not gotten with the program! Many times I have visited beautiful establishments where the only vegetarian item on the menu was pasta with marinara sauce.

The other problem I find is that many entrées that restaurants consider to be vegetarian are covered in cheese or made with a cream sauce. Ayurveda has nothing against dairy and even recommends it in some cases. But remember that the Ayurvedic texts were written five thousand years ago when there were no alternatives to dairy. Now we have such great products, made with either rice or soy, from which we can get the benefits and the taste of dairy without the digestive problems that can accompany it. Many people are lactose intolerant and simply cannot process dairy in their digestive tracts. Because of the options available to us now, this is no longer a problem!

When ordering in a restaurant, if there is nothing on the menu that fits into the vegan category, I simply state my case to the waiter and see what the chef can come up with. If enough of us speak up instead of trying to make do with a salad or a side of French fries, things will eventually change. A true vegetarian diet technically prohibits eggs, but there are so many things (like breads) that have eggs in them that I have found that it is better not to strain and just go with it, rather than to try to avoid eggs altogether. When cooking at home, we have the option of using egg substitutes or egg replacers if we choose to do so.

I believe in having a good time in the kitchen, so I don't get caught up in exact measurements or specific ingredients. Use foods, spices, and smells that you like—be creative, improvise! Consider cooking to be an art rather than a science.

I have found that cooking at home can be easy, fast, and fun! Using some convenience foods really cuts down on prep time. I've come up with a bunch of different recipes that incorporate what I've learned from Ayurvedic cooking, with an American palate (well, Australian, too, since my husband is from Australia) that craves variety. And I've figured out ways to cook that save me lots of time and money, too. The best part is that by cooking at home, you're taking care of yourself and you know exactly what you're eating. The added benefit is that it's a wonderful way to show the people in your life how much you love them.

RECIPES
TO FEED YOUR DOSHA

BLUEBERRY MUFFINS

✦

MAKES 12 EXTRA-LARGE MUFFINS

2 cups flour
1 cup sugar
¼ teaspoon salt
3 teaspoons baking powder
1 cup fresh blueberries
2 eggs (or the equivalent in egg substitutes)
1 cup buttermilk (or vanilla soy milk)
2 teaspoons vanilla
½ cup unsalted (sweet) butter or margarine, melted

1. Preheat oven to 350°F. Mix the flour, sugar, salt, and baking powder together in a large bowl. When thoroughly combined, add the fresh blueberries. (The flour coats the berries so they don't sink to the bottom of the batter.)
2. In a separate bowl, mix together the eggs, buttermilk, vanilla, and butter. Make a hole in the center of the dry ingredients, pour in the wet ingredients, and mix together just until moist; don't overmix!
3. Scoop into muffin cups lined with paper, or greased muffin tins, and bake for approximately 40 minutes, or until golden brown.

VARIATION: Instead of blueberries, add dried cranberries and chopped walnuts, and substitute orange peel for the vanilla. The blueberry version is great for Vatas; the cranberry version is especially good for Kaphas.

SAMOSAS

✦

MAKES 12 SAMOSAS

SAMOSAS ARE LIKE little hot sandwiches. This is another great recipe where you can make a whole bunch at one time and freeze some for later. I freeze them individually and then pull them out when I need a quick lunch. I make two different versions, one Indian (with coconut milk for Pittas), one Greek—see which you like best!

2 boxes frozen Pepperidge Farm Puff Pastry, thawed

Indian filling
2 or 3 potatoes, baked, skinned, and chopped
1 can (14 ounces) lite coconut milk
1 cup frozen peas, thawed
Curry powder to taste (1–3 tablespoons, depending how spicy you like it)

Greek filling
1 bag (10 ounces) frozen chopped spinach, thawed
1 bag (8 ounces) shredded soy mozzarella or Monterey Jack cheese
1 package (12 ounces) Mori Nu lite firm silken tofu
1–2 tablespoons nutmeg

1. Preheat the oven to 350°F. Spray nonstick shortening on two cookie sheets.
2. Open the pastry boxes: you'll see that there are two sheets of pastry. Each sheet is folded into thirds. Cut the pastry along those lines. Each third of a sheet will be one samosa.
3. Choose a filling and mix all ingredients together in a medium-size bowl.
4. Drop the filling on the bottom half of the pastry, fold the top half over, and pinch the three open sides closed. Each filling recipe makes enough for 12 samosas.
5. Bake for 30 minutes or until the pastry is golden brown and flaky.

TOMATO–VEGETABLE PASTA SAUCE

MAKES 12 GENEROUS SERVINGS

THIS RECIPE MAKE a lot of sauce—you can easily have a hefty portion for dinner and then fill four or five glass jars to freeze for later. There are tastes in here for every dosha—and the white beans add protein.

¼ cup olive oil
1 onion, diced
1 tablespoon chopped garlic
1 eggplant, chopped into bite-size pieces
1 large zucchini, chopped into bite-size pieces
1 yellow squash, chopped into bite-size pieces
1 large bunch of fresh basil leaves, chopped
3 cans (28 ounces) tomato sauce
1 can (28 ounces) crushed tomatoes
1 can (11 ounces) tomato paste
1 can (15 ounces) small white beans
1 tablespoon sugar
1 cup red wine

1. On medium-high heat, brown the onion and garlic in the olive oil in a large pot. Add the chopped vegetables and basil, and sauté until soft. Then add all the tomato sauce, crushed tomatoes, tomato paste, and beans and stir until well blended.
2. Add the sugar and the wine, stir well, and simmer on low for 20 minutes or so.
3. Serve over your favorite pasta. This works really well over rigatoni; it's chunky and easy to eat.

PESTO PASTA SAUCE

MAKES 12 GENEROUS SERVINGS

YOU CAN MAKE this in a food processor or a blender; whatever is easier for you. Basil is good for both Vata and Kapha.

1 bag (12 ounces) already-washed baby spinach leaves
1 large bunch of fresh basil leaves
⅓ cup olive oil
¼ cup sunflower seeds
soy Parmesan, for garnish
pine nuts, for garnish

1. Place all of the ingredients in a food processor or blender and mix.
2. Toss in a bowl with hot pasta. Add soy Parmesan or pine nuts on top (optional). I like this with penne rigate or butterfly pasta—something textured, where the pesto can cling to the noodles.

DIVINE DA VINCI SAUCE

MAKES 4 GENEROUS SERVINGS

THIS SAUCE LOOKS really fancy. It's totally easy, yet makes any meal seem like a special occasion! It's a work of art!

3 tablespoons butter or margarine
1 teaspoon chopped or minced garlic
1 tablespoon flour
⅓ cup vegetable broth
½ bag (5 ounces) already-washed baby spinach leaves
1 can or jar (6 ounces) artichoke hearts cut into slivers
1 small bag (3–4 ounces) pine nuts
2 large tomatoes, diced
¼ cup white wine
1 tablespoon lemon juice

1. In a large frying pan, over medium heat, melt the butter, and then add the garlic. Add the flour and mix well.
2. Pour in the vegetable broth and continue stirring. Next add the spinach leaves, and keep stirring until they all get limp. Add in the artichoke hearts and pine nuts, and then finally the tomatoes.
3. When it is all heated up, add the wine and the lemon juice, and cook another couple of minutes. Serve over pasta. This looks really pretty over angel hair or thin spaghetti.

Chinese Chicken Salad . . . Without the Chicken!

Makes 6 generous servings

Salads are wonderful for Pittas, and with all the extra goodies in here, this salad is filling and tasty!

Dressing:
½ cup sesame oil
¼ cup seasoned rice vinegar
2 tablespoons sugar
1 tablespoon sesame seeds

1 cup uncooked jasmine rice, cooked per directions
1 head romaine lettuce, chopped
2 heads butter lettuce, chopped
1 large can (15 ounces) mandarin oranges, drained
1 can (8 ounces) sliced water chestnuts, drained
1 cup bean sprouts
½ cup chopped green onions
½ can (5 ounces) chow mein noodles
cherry, grape, or pear tomatoes, optional
avocado, optional
tofu chicken strips, optional
bamboo shoots, optional

1. Heat the dressing on the stove just until the sugar dissolves.
2. Mix all of your favorite ingredients from the list above in a large bowl.
3. Toss with the dressing until well covered.

PICNIC SALAD

✦

I CALL THIS the picnic salad because it's the one we always take with us when we go on a picnic! The avocado is good for Vatas and Pittas. Just bring a loaf of sourdough along and you've got a hearty meal.

1 package (16 ounces) mini-rigatoni or other bite-sized pasta,
cooked per directions on package
1 head romaine or red leaf lettuce, chopped
1 small bag (3–4 ounces) pine nuts, toasted
1–2 tomatoes, chopped
1 avocado, chopped
½ cup shredded soy Parmesan/romano cheese
1 cup garlic/butter croutons

Dressing:
½ cup olive oil
¼ cup balsamic or red wine vinegar

1. Mix salad ingredients in a large bowl.
2. Toss with dressing.

TOSTADA SALAD

MAKES 4 GENERAL SERVINGS

THIS RECIPE IS great for parties. I like to set out big bowls of all the ingredients so guests can just go down the line filling their shells with anything they want.

1 package burrito-size flour tortillas
1 can (16 ounces) vegetarian refried beans, heated
6.75 ounce box Spanish rice (I like Far East brand; 1 box serves 4)
1 handful chopped lettuce
8 ounces shredded soy Monterey Jack and/or cheddar cheese
1 tomato, chopped
1 cup cooked corn
black olives, sliced
1 avocado, chopped
1 tablespoon picante sauce
1 tablespoon salsa
1 tablespoon soy sour cream

1. Line an oven-safe bowl with tortillas and bake at 400°F for 15 minutes, to make the shell for the salad.
2. While the tortilla shell "bowl" is still warm, layer from the bottom up the beans (about 2 heaping tablespoons per tostada), 1 scoop of rice, lettuce, and toppings.
3. Have some little bowls filled with picante sauce, salsa, and/or sour cream on the table for added zest and garnish.

LISA'S LASAGNA

MAKES 8 TO 10 SERVINGS

I'VE MADE THIS for lots of parties, and people are surprised when they find out that this is made with tofu and soy cheese instead of the real thing. It's my dad's favorite! Both Ronzoni and Barrilla make great no-boil lasagna noodles. You'll need one box of either brand.

1 box (12 ounces) Mori Nu firm silken tofu
1 egg (or 2 egg whites), lightly beaten
1 teaspoon garlic powder
2 jars (52 ounces) of your favorite spaghetti sauce, or make your own
(I get mine at an Italian deli
so it tastes totally homemade without the extra effort!)
1 box (8–9 ounces) pre-cooked lasagna noodles
1 bag (5 ounces) already-washed baby spinach leaves, steamed
(you can microwave them right in the bag)
2 bags (16 ounces) shredded soy mozzarella cheese
2 teaspoons pine nuts, toasted

1. Mix together the silken tofu, egg, and garlic powder and set aside. This is your "faux ricotta" cheese.
2. Spray a 13 x 9-inch baking pan with nonstick shortening and spoon some spaghetti sauce into the bottom of the pan.
3. Lay three noodles on top of the sauce side by side, spoon more sauce over the noodles, and sprinkle cheese over the sauce.
4. Continue layering this way, adding the spinach to one layer, and the faux ricotta to another layer, until you run out of noodles or reach the top of the pan.
5. Finish with a layer of cheese on the top, and sprinkle with toasted pine nuts (optional).
6. Cover with foil and bake according to directions on noodle box. (The time will be different, depending on which noodles you use.)

STIR FRY WITH ALMOND SAUCE

IT DOESN'T REALLY matter which vegetables you use—choose whichever you like the best, what works for your dosha, or what's in season. Add some tofu, slivered almonds, sesame seeds, bamboo shoots, whatever you have on hand. Stir-fry the vegetables in a large wok, using just a small amount of sesame oil. The sauce is what makes this dish so special. You could use peanut butter instead of the almond butter, but almonds are so Vata-pacifying that I use them whenever I can. Plus, many people are allergic to peanuts, including me! This recipe makes a big batch of sauce because I like to freeze it in jars to keep on hand. It's so easy to just heat up the sauce, boil some jasmine rice, and stir-fry some veggies. It's a complete meal, and so yummy!

Almond Sauce
1 jar (16 ounces) almond butter
1 cup rice vinegar
¾ cup Bragg's liquid aminos (or lite soy sauce)
2 cans (14 ounces) lite coconut milk
1 can (15 ounces) Coco Lopez Cream of Coconut
½ cup dark brown sugar
1½ teaspoons ground cumin
1½ teaspoons ground coriander
¼ cup garlic purée
3 cups almond or sesame oil

1. Combine all ingredients in a frying pan over low heat; whisk well.
2. Pour into jars and cool completely. Freeze until ready for use.

POTATO FRITTATA

·✦·

SERVES 4 TO 6

THERE'S TOFU AND soy cheese in this dish—lots of protein. Turmeric is really good for Kaphas.

1 pound firm tofu, crumbled (you can use silken tofu, if you prefer)
¼ cup soy milk
3 tablespoons parsley flakes
¼ teaspoon turmeric
½ cup shredded soy mozzarella cheese
1 tablespoon olive oil
1 teaspoon chopped or minced garlic
1 bag (16 ounces) diced potatoes, or 2 large potatoes baked and diced

1. Preheat oven to 400°F.
2. Place half the tofu in a food processor or blender, along with the soy milk, parsley, turmeric, and half of the soy cheese. Blend until smooth and set aside.
3. Heat the oil in a large frying pan over medium heat. Add the garlic and potatoes and sauté until the potatoes are lightly brown, about 5 minutes.
4. Add the remaining tofu and the blended tofu mix, stirring well. Cook for about 5 minutes, or until it begins to get firm.
5. Shift the frittata into a baking pan and top with the rest of the cheese.
6. Bake in the oven for 20–25 minutes, or until firm and hot, then remove from oven and let stand for 10 minutes.

SMOOTHIES

WE USE THE blender every day at our house, and everyone has a favorite smoothie! They're just so simple to whip up, and so delicious! You pick the portion sizes depending on how much you want to drink. Following are combinations that make about two smoothies in one blender.

Here's my favorite—great for Vatas!
¼ cup blueberries
1 banana
½ papaya
2 cups vanilla soy milk
1 container (4 ounces) mango soy pudding

Pitta smoothie
4–6 strawberries (depending on size)
½ cup pineapple
1 can (14 ounces) lite coconut milk
1½ cups ice

Kapha smoothie
1 apple, cut up
1 pear, cut up
2 cups apple juice (may be frozen in summer, to make it cooler!)
1 teaspoon cinnamon

There are so many great combinations—consider mixing and matching any of these ingredients to create your own original smoothies:

Silken tofu	Mango	Orange juice	Almonds
Protein powder	Kiwi	Prune juice	
Peach	Apricot	Chocolate soy pudding	
Melon	Plum	Banana soy pudding	

Afterword

L IVING LIFE THE Vedic way is basically about living life in love. It's all about love! Love takes on myriad forms in all its glorious expressions: love for your family, your friends, your work, your home, your world, and yourself. Love is all around you, love is what we are all made of; you just have to open yourself up to it. When you connect with others, when you see the beauty of your relationships, you are free to experience and to express more of that love . . . and to experience and express more of yourself. This is our purpose as human beings, this is our joy.

Here we are, two people and yet
One.
I see who you are,
And I know who I am.

With this glimpse of
Clarity and peace
Comes the grace
Of the moment,
The joy of true love.

Live well, eat well, love well. Spend time in silence and gratitude. Learn and grow. Be who you are, and know who that is. Dance the dance.

Thank you for sharing this time with me.

Namaste and love,

Lisa Marie

GLOSSARY OF SANSKRIT
WORDS & TERMS

SANSKRIT WORDS HAVE many layers of meaning. The following are definitions based on how these words are used in the context of this book.

A̅

AGNI: Fire
AHAMKARA: Ego
ANANDA: Bliss
ANNA: Food
ANNAPURNA: Goddess of food
ASANAS: Yoga postures
AYURVEDA: "Science of life"

B̅

BHAKTI: Devotion
BHAKTI YOGA: The path of love
BUDHA: Mercury

C̅

CHAKRA: "Wheel." Also, a spiritual center located in the
   subtle body
CHANDRA: The moon

$\overline{D}$

DHATU: Tissue

DOSHA: A functional quality, metabolic principle. Vata, Pitta, or Kapha

$\overline{G}$

GANDHA: The sense of smell

GRAHA: Planet

GURU: Jupiter

$\overline{J}$

JNANA YOGA: The path of knowledge

JYOTISH: Vedic astrology. "The study of light"

$\overline{K}$

KAMA SUTRA: "The science of love." Ancient text written by the Vedic sage Vatyayana over two thousand years ago

KAPHA: One of the functional qualities in Ayurveda. Kapha is composed of earth and water

KARMA: Action, and the result of action

KARMA YOGA: The path of work

KETU: South node of the moon

$\overline{M}$

MAHAT: Intelligence

MALA: String of 108 or 54 beads used in Mantra practice.

MANGALA: Mars

MANTRA: Sanskrit syllables combined for various purposes. Instrument of the mind

MERU BEAD: The dangling bead on a mala which marks the starting point for Mantra practice

MOKSHA: Ecstasy

N̲

NAMASTE: Sanskrit greeting. "The divine in me honors the divine in you"

O̲

OM: A mantra in itself. No literal translation. Oneness, the universal

P̲

PITTA: One of the functional qualities in Ayurveda. Pitta is composed of fire and water

PRAKRITI: Material

PRAKRUTI: Primordial matter. Constitution. Balance

PRANA: Breath. Life force

PRANAYAMA: Yogic breathing exercises

PUJA: Prayer

PURUSHA: Consciousness. Spirit

R̲

RAHU: North node of the moon

RAJAS: Electrons

RAJA YOGA: The path of meditation

RASA: The sense of taste. Also juice, emotion

RASAYANA: Recommendation, remedy

RUPA: The sense of sight

S̲

SABDA: The sense of hearing

SANSKRIT: Vedic language. Mantras are written in Sanskrit

SAHASRARA: The seventh chakra; also called the crown chakra

SATTVAS: Protons

SPARSA: The sense of touch

SAT: Truth (also called *satyam*)

SEVA: Service

SHAKTI: Feminine power or energy
SHANI: Saturn
SHANTI: Peace
SHIVA: Masculine energy. Also, consciousness
SIDDHA: A sage
SUKRA: Venus
SURYA: The sun

T̲

TAMAS: Neutrons
TANTRA: Instrument of the body. Technique. Also, the joining of masculine and feminine energies

U̲

UPANISHADS: Sacred Vedic philosophical texts

V̲

VAIDYA: An Ayurvedic doctor
VASTU: Dwelling or site. Science for enhancing our environment
VATA: One of the functional qualities in Ayurveda. Vata is composed of air and space
VATSYAYANA: Vedic sage, author of *Kama Sutra*
VIKRUTI: Altered state of doshas. Imbalance

Y̲

YOGA: To unite. Also, techniques for developing and integrating energy

REFERENCES & RECOMMENDED READING

Ashley-Farrand, Thomas. *Healing Mantras: Using Sound Affirmations for Personal Power, Creativity, and Healing.* New York, NY: Ballantine-Wellspring, 1999.

Barks, Coleman. *Birdsong, Rumi.* Athens, GA: Maypop, 1993.

Barks, Coleman with Moyne, John. *The Essential Rumi.* Edison, NJ: Castle Books, 1997.

Bragg, Gina Bell and Simon, M.D., David. *A Simple Celebration: A Vegetarian Cookbook for Body, Mind, and Spirit.* New York, NY: Harmony Books, 1997.

Carroll, Cain and Kimata, Lori, N.D. *Partner Yoga: Making Contact for Physical, Emotional, and Spiritual Growth.* Emmaus, PA: Rodale/Reach, 2000.

Carter-Scott, Cherie. *If Love Is a Game, These Are the Rules: Ten Rules for Finding Love and Creating Long-Lasting Authentic Relationships.* New York, NY: Broadway Books, 1999.

Chatterji, J.C. *The Wisdom of the Vedas.* Wheaton, IL: The Theosophical Publishing House, 1992.

Chopra, Deepak. *The Love Poems of Rumi.* London, England: Rider/Random House, 1998.

Chopra, M.D., Deepak. The *Path to Love: Spiritual Strategies for Healing.* New York, NY: Three Rivers Press, 1997.

Chopra, M.D., Deepak. *Perfect Health: The Complete Mind/Body Guide.* New York, NY: Harmony Books, 1991.

Chopra, M.D., Deepak, et al. *The Chopra Center Cookbook: Nourishing Body and Soul.* Hoboken, NJ: John Wiley & Sons, 2002.

Chopra, M.D., Krishan. *The Mystery and Magic of Love.* Carlsbad, CA: Hay House, Inc., 2001.

Cox, Kathleen. *Vastu Living: Creating a Home for the Soul.* New York, NY: Marlowe & Company, 2000.

Davis, Roy Eugene. *An Easy Guide to Ayurveda: The Natural Way to Wholeness.* Lakemont, GA: CSA Press, 1996.

De Fouw, Hart and Svoboda, Robert E. *Light on Relationships: The Synastry of Indian Astrology.* York Beach, ME: Samuel Weiser, Inc., 2000.

Ford, Debbie. *Spiritual Divorce: Divorce as a Catalyst for an Extrordinary Life.* San Francisco, CA: Harper San Francisco, 2001.

Frawley, David. *Tantric Yoga and the Wisdom Goddesses.* Salt Lake City, UT: Passage Press, 1994.

Frawley, David. *Yoga & Ayurveda: Self-Healing and Self-Realization.* Twin Lakes, WI: Lotus Press, 1999.

Hospodar, Miriam Kasin. *Heaven's Banquet: Vegetarian Cooking for Lifelong Health the Ayurveda Way.* New York, NY: Dutton, 1999.

Iyengar, B.K.S. *Light on Pranayama: The Yogic Art of Breathing.* New York, NY: Crossroad Publishing Company, 2002.

Johari, Harish. *Ayurvedic Massage: Traditional Indian Techniques for Balancing Body and Mind.* Rochester, VT: Healing Arts Press, 1996.

Johari, Harish. *The Healing Cuisine: India's Art of Ayurvedic Cooking.* Rochester, VT: Healing Arts Press, 1994.

Khalsa, M.D., Dharma Singh and Stauth, Cameron. *Meditation as Medicine: Activate the Power of Your Natural Healing Force.* New York, NY: Pocket Books, 2001.

Kirby, Connie and Robert Dunne, with Ross, Geraldine. *The Art of Sensual Yoga.* New York, NY: Plume, 1997.

Lad, Vasant. *The Complete Book of Ayurvedic Home Remedies.* New York, NY: Three Rivers Press, 1998.

Lad, Vasant. *Textbook of Ayurveda: Fundamental Principles.* Albuquerque, NM: The Ayurvedic Press, 2002.

Ladinsky, Daniel. *Love Poems from God: Twelve Sacred Voices from the East and West.* New York, NY: Penguin Compass, 2002.

Levacy, William R. *Beneath a Vedic Sky: A Beginner's Guide to the Astrology of Ancient India.* Carlsbad, CA: Hay House, 1999.

Marshall, Henry. *Mantras: A Musical Path to Peace.* Woodside, CA: Bluestar Communications, 1999.

Morningstar, Amadea with Desai, Urmila. *The Ayurvedic Cookbook: A Personalized Guide to Good Nutrition and Health.* Wilmot, WI: Lotus Light Publishing, 1991.

Moyne, John and Barks, Coleman. *Unseen Rain, Quatrains of Rumi.* Putney, VT: Threshold Books, 1986.

Odier, Daniel. *Desire: The Tantric Path to Awakening.* Rochester, VT: Inner Traditions, 2001.

Radha, Swami Sivananda. *Mantras: Words of Power.* Spokane, WA: Timeless Books, 1994.

Raichur, Pratima with Cohn, Marian. *Absolute Beauty: Radiant Skin and Inner Harmony Through the Ancient Secrets of Ayurveda.* New York, NY: HarperCollins Publishers, 1997.

Shiva, Shahram. *Hush, Don't Say Anything to God: Passionate Poems of Rumi.* Freemont, CA: Jain Publishing Company, 2000.

Tirtha, Swami Sada Shiva. *The Ayurvedic Encyclopedia: Natural Secrets to Healing, Prevention, & Longevity.* Bayville, NY: Ayurveda Holistic Center Press, 1998.

Too, Lillian. *Mantras & Mudras: Meditations for the Hands and Voice to Bring Peace and Inner Calm*. Hammersmith, London: Element, 2002.

Tripurari, Swami B.V. *Aesthetic Vedanta: The Sacred Path of Passionate Love*. Eugene, OR: Mandala Publishing Group, 1998.

Tripurari, Swami B.V. *Rasa: Love Relationships in Transcendence*. Eugene, OR: Clarion Call Publishing, 1994.

Vrajaprana, Pravrajika. *Vedanta: A Simple Introduction*. Hollywood, CA: Vedanta Press, 1999.

Williamson, Marianne. *Enchanted Love: The Mystical Power of Intimate Relationships*. New York, NY: Touchstone, 1999.

ACKNOWLEDGMENTS

T HE STUDY OF AYURVEDA, and living the Ayurvedic lifestyle, has completely changed my life. I must thank Louise Taylor, my first teacher and dear friend, for introducing me to the subject. Thank you also to Deepak Chopra, who has expanded my awareness and brought me to Vedanta, and to India. My sincere gratitude to my friends and colleagues at The Chopra Center at the La Costa Resort, especially Carolyn Rangel, David Simon, Roger Gabriel, Brent Becvar, Leanne Backer, Corrine Champigny, David Greenspan, and my fellow meditation teachers and students.

A warm thank you to Vasant Lad, who has been so generous with his wisdom and teachings, and brought so much to the world with his work. And thank you to Wynn Werner at the Ayurvedic Institute in Albuquerque, New Mexico, for his guidance.

Thank you hugs to Barbara Neighbors Deal, my wonderful agent, for her support and confidence in this project. And thank you to Caroline Pincus, "book midwife," for her help all along the way. Everyone at Marlowe has been so fabulous to work with—bouquets of gratitude to Sue McCloskey and Matthew Lore.

There are so many people in my life who have taught me about the real value of relationships. Thank you to my friends and family, from whom I learn every day. Thank you to Freddy and Brian, and to Ryan, Ellen and Annika, for bringing light from California to Australia and all around the world!

Thank you kisses to my husband, Greg, who shows me time and time again how precious and perfect love really is.

And thank you, dear readers, for understanding the importance of love and relationships in our lives. Through the lessons of Ayurveda, we can learn and grow together, and become happier, more peaceful, and more loving friends and partners and people!

INDEX